18815

FRANKLIN DELANO ROOSEVELT
1882 - 1945

Edited by
Howard F. Bremer

Series Editor
Howard F. Bremer

1971
OCEANA PUBLICATIONS, INC.
Dobbs Ferry, New York 10522

Library of Congress Catalog Card Number: 71-116062
International Standard Book Number: 0-379-12066-6

Manufactured in the United States of America

CONTENTS

Editor's Foreword

The Presidential Chronology series is a research tool compiled primarily for the student. The combination of chronological events with important messages and a critical bibliography should aid students as well as their advising teachers and librarians, in searching for additional materials on which to study the important events in each administration, and to write better research papers as a result.

Scholars already adept in research might also find the Chronology useful. Every effort has been made to insure accuracy and to include as many important events and names as feasible in these little volumes.

The period of Franklin D. Roosevelt posed especial problems for the editor. He was at first surprised on being told at the Franklin D. Roosevelt Library at Hyde Park that it had no chronology on F.D.R. Now he knows why. It is an impossible job. Something, somebody, has to be left out. So with thanks to all those who helped search for the more important items at the Hyde Park Library, particularly Joseph Marshall, to other Roosevelt scholars who pointed the way to significance and meaning, and to all "New Dealers" somehow left out I respectfully dedicate this book.

I am especially indebted to Miss Carolyn Peoples for the preparation of the name index, and to my wife, Helene, and daughter Wendy for their hours of typing, their critical comments, and their patient proofreading.

The documents printed here are taken from Franklin D. Roosevelt, The Public Papers and Addresses, edited by Samuel Rosenman.

CHRONOLOGY

YOUTH

1882

January 30   Born: Hyde Park, New York. Father: James; Mother: Sara Delano.

March 20   Christened at St. James Episcopal Church in Hyde Park. Godparents were William Howard Forbes, brother-in-law of Sarah Delano Roosevelt, and friends Eleanor Blodgett and Elliott Roosevelt. Elliott married Anna Hall later that year and their daughter, Anna Eleanor, born October 11, 1884, was to become Mrs. Franklin D. Roosevelt.

1886

Spent summer at Campobello as family became permanent residents on land purchased in 1883.

1888

October 22   Formal education started under a governess of Archibald and Edmund Rogers, Fraulein Reinhardt, learning some German.

1889

Went abroad in summer, coming down with a mild case of typhoid fever. Convalesced in England.

1890-91

Tutored by a Miss Riensberg at Hyde Park.

September 28   Began studies under a Swiss governess, Mlle. Jeanne Sardoz for two years, learning some French and English, and perhaps some social consciousness which led him to sympathize with the masses even at this early age.

1

1891

May   In Bad Nauheim, Germany, for family's annual cure.
               Attended German public school for a time.

1893-1896

               Studied under private tutors, including Arthur Dumper
               who stayed longest.

1896

September   Entered Groton School. Headmaster, Endicott Peabody.

1897

February 25   Made what was probably his first political speech while
               debating at Groton. Spoke two minutes on the Nicaragua
               Canal Bill.

July 2   Visited Oyster Bay to stay with Theodore Roosevelt for
               weekend before going to Campobello.

September   Entered fourth form at Groton.

December 25   Received Alfred Thayer Mahan's Influence of Sea Power
               Upon History from relatives, indicating his interest in
               the sea and naval power.

1898

January 17   Death of grandfather, Warren Delano II.

January 19   Delivered address upholding negative during debate:
               "Resolved, that Hawaii be promptly annexed."

January 30   Received Alfred Thayer Mahan's latest book, The
               Interest of America in Sea Power, Present and Future
               as a birthday present.

April 22   Beginning of war with Spain excited Franklin, but he
               was apparently not an expansionist.

April   Scarlet fever isolated him at Groton, and then led to a
               convalescence at Hyde Park.

November   Father, a Democrat, supported Theodore Roosevelt
                  for Governor of New York. "Teddy's" victory made
                  Franklin "wild with delight," all "proving" that blood
                  is thicker than politics.

1899

May 16   Letter to parents commented that a lecturer at Groton
                  (Professor Edward S. Morse) "ran down the poor China-
                  men a little too much and thought too much of the Japs."

September   Began last (sixth form) year at Groton.

1900

June 25   Was graduated from Groton with a B average and award-
                  ed the Latin prize.

September   Entered Harvard. Tried out for football and crew,
                  rather unsuccessfully. More successful on Harvard
                  Crimson: elected an editor for the following June.

December 8   Death of father, James Roosevelt after long illness with
                  a heart condition.

1901

Theodore Roosevelt, cousin, became President of the
United States upon death of William McKinley. Franklin learned news upon return from a European tour with
his mother and two friends.

1902

Mother took apartment in Boston to be near Franklin.

1903

September   Returned to Harvard for senior year; elected president
                  (editor-in-chief) of the Crimson.

November   Became engaged to Eleanor Roosevelt, daughter of
                  Elliott (a brother of Theodore Roosevelt) and Anna Hall
                  Roosevelt. Elliott had been one of Franklin's god-
                  parents.

1904

June
Graduated from Harvard without distinction in scholarship but with considerable success in social and in extracurricular activities.

Entered the Columbia University School of Law. Never completed courses for the LL.B degree but did pass New York Bar Examination in 1906.

1905

March 17
Married Eleanor at adjoining homes of Eleanor's cousin, Susie Parish, and Mrs. Parish's mother, Mrs. E. Livingston Low, on East 76th Street in New York City. The Reverend Endicott Peabody of Groton performed the ceremony and President Theodore Roosevelt gave away his niece in marriage.

June 7
The newlyweds took a three month delayed honeymoon trip to Europe.

1906

May 3
Birth of first child, Anna Eleanor Roosevelt, in New York City.

EARLY CAREER

1907

September
Joined law firm of Carter, Ledyard and Milburn, 54 Wall Street, in New York City.

December 23
James, first son, born in New York City.

1908

March 18
Franklin Delano, Jr., born. Died November 8, 1909.

1910

September 23
Elliott, second surviving son, born in New York City.

October 6
Nominated by Democrats for state senator from New York's 26th District.

1910

Oct. 7-Nov. 7   Campaigned strenuously, touring rural areas in a red
                  Maxwell, stressing themes of clean government and
                  antibossism.

November 8   Elected to New York State Senate, receiving 15,708
                  votes to his Republican opponent, John F. Schlosser's
                  14,568.

1911

January 1   Took first public office as state senator, moving with
                  family to Albany, New York.

January 16   At a Democratic caucus took leadership of a group of
                  insurgents who were fighting to prevent a Tammany
                  candidate, William F. Sheehan, from being named
                  United States Senator.

March 31   Three month fight ended with selection of a compromise
                  candidate, James A. O'Gorman, still a Tammany leader.
                  Roosevelt had become well-known in his state with this
                  battle against bossism.

July 24   Legislature began summer recess and F.D.R. spent
                  summer at Campobello.

December   First meeting with Governor Woodrow Wilson at Trent-
                  on, New Jersey.

1912

January   Led fight for conservation measures but was blocked
                  by Tammany tactics.

April-May   Visited Jamaica, and then Panama to see the canal under
                  construction.

June   Played minor role at Democratic convention in Balti-
                  more supporting Woodrow Wilson's nomination for the
                  presidency.

July 17   Organized The Empire State Democracy with seventy other progressives to support Wilson's campaign and to oppose Tammany's domination of the state ticket.

August 24   Renominated for the state senate. Unable to campaign because he contracted typhoid fever, obtained services of Louis McHenry Howe, a newspaperman, to run campaign for him.

November 5   Reelected to state senate in spite of illness and attacks from Tammany.

1913

Jan. 1-Mar. 17   In second term as senator introduced five bills to aid farmers.

March 17   Appointed Assistant Secretary of the Navy by President Wilson, serving under Secretary Josephus Daniels.

April 10   Speech before Navy League in Washington, D.C. stresses need for a large navy. F.D.R. made many speeches on this and other themes while Assistant Secretary.

1914

April   Statements to the press while on a Western tour indicate a bellicose attitude toward Mexico.

August 13   Announced candidacy in the Democratic primary for United States Senator from New York.

August 17   Franklin Delano, Jr., born at Campobello, New Brunswick, Canada.

September   Tammany nominated James Gerard, Ambassador to Germany, to run against F.D.R.

September 11   Began campaign in New York State. Gerard did not campaign, remaining in Germany.

September 29   Lost in primary by a decisive margin, almost three to
                    one, but did reasonably well upstate, away from Tam-
                    many-controlled New York City.

                    During the year Lucy Mercer came to work as a sec-
                    retary to Mrs. Roosevelt. F.D.R., for a time, at
                    least, was attracted to her.

                               1915
                    An undated letter to Mrs. Roosevelt, but undoubtedly
                    written early in 1915, stated: "I just <u>know</u> I shall do
                    some unneutral thing before I get through!"

                               1916
March 2   John Aspinwall, youngest son, born in Washington, D.C.

November 8   "The most extraordinary day of my life." This was
                    Roosevelt's reaction the day after Woodrow Wilson's
                    close reelection.

                               1917
January 21   Left Washington on inspection tour of Haiti and Santo
                    Domingo.

February 3   Received word from Secretary Daniels while in Santo
                    Domingo to return to Washington. Germany had an-
                    nounced (January 31) its intention to resume unrestricted
                    submarine warfare.

April 2   Heard Wilson's war message to Congress. War against
                    Germany was voted April 6.

July 4   Gave main address at the Tammany "Wigwam" in New
                    York City, making his peace with Boss Murphy. He
                    was apparently being groomed for governor.

November   Roosevelt's plan for a North Sea mine barrage approved,
                    after long opposition from some Navy officials in the
                    United States and the British Admirality.

1918

July 9   Left Brooklyn on a destroyer for an inspection trip in
                 Europe. Inspected installations in England, came un-
                 der fire in France, and tried his hand at diplomacy in
                 Italy.

September 19   Arrived in New York on the Leviathan, seriously ill
                 with influenza.

October 15   Finally well enough to resume duties in Washington and
                 report to Secretary Daniels on his European inspection
                 tour.

1919

January 1   Sailed with Mrs. Roosevelt on the George Washington
                 for Europe on mission to dismantle American Navy
                 installations.

February 24   Arrived in Boston on George Washington, which also
                 brought President Wilson back from the Peace Confer-
                 ence. A luncheon meeting with Wilson had convinced
                 Roosevelt that the United States must join the League
                 of Nations.

May 29   In speech before the Democratic National Committee
                 in Chicago, claimed that the progressive movement in
                 the Republican Party had died.

June 25   In Commencement Address at Worcester Polytechnic
                 Institute said that there would be many crises in inter-
                 national affairs for many years to come. "In them the
                 United States cannot escape an important, perhaps even
                 a controlling voice."

July 20   Attempt made by Republican senators to involve F.D.R.
                 in a Navy scandal at Newport, charging that he had
                 authorized highly objectionable methods in collecting
                 evidence in homosexual cases. The charges were ob-
                 viously partisan and soon ignored.

July   Serious riots in Washington, D.C. between Negroes
                        and Whites lasted several days. The Army Reserve
                        finally was called in. Roosevelt wished quicker action
                        had been taken, but generally did not support the Red
                        baiters of the day.

                                        1920
June 26   At opening sessions of Democratic National Convention
                        made headlines by inviting delegates to visit battleship
                        New York, then in San Francisco; the next day by seiz-
                        ing New York's standard from reluctant Tammany lead-
                        ers and joining parade demonstrating in support of
                        Woodrow Wilson.

June 30   Seconded the nomination of Alfred E. Smith for Presi-
                        dent.

July 6   Received Democratic nomination for Vice President to
                        run with Governor James M. Cox of Ohio.

July 18   With Governor Cox met with the ailing President Wilson
                        at the White House. Cox promised to make support
                        for the League the paramount issue of the campaign.

August 6   Resigned position of Assistant Secretary of the Navy.

August 9   Received formal notification at Hyde Park of nomination
                        for the Vice Presidency.

August 11   Started campaign in Chicago.

August 18   At Butte, Montana, boasted that he had written Haiti's
                        constitution himself, thus giving the Republicans an
                        excellent campaign issue.

November 2   Harding and Coolidge won, receiving 16 million votes
                        to Cox and Roosevelt's 9 million, and 404 electoral
                        votes to 127.

November   Miss Marguerite ("Missy") Le Hand became his private
                    secretary.

                               1921

January 1   Returned to law practice with the firm of Emmet,
                    Marvin and Roosevelt. Also named vice president of
                    the Fidelity and Deposit Company of Maryland in charge
                    of New York office.

August 10   While at Campobello contracted infantile paralysis
                    (poliomyelitis).

September 15   Taken to Presbyterian Hospital in New York City.

October 28   Went home to his house on 65th Street in New York City.

                               1922

February   Began use of leg braces of steel, weighing seven pounds
                    each.

June   Became president of the American Construction Coun-
                    cil, a trade association to provide self-regulation of
                    the building industry, including codes of ethics and
                    price agreements. Kept position until 1928.

August 13   Wrote an open letter which made front page news ap-
                    pealing to Alfred E. Smith to seek the governorship of
                    New York.

September   From Hyde Park worked to support Al Smith and to
                    keep William Randolph Hearst, who was seeking either
                    the governorship or senatorship, off the ticket.

November   Al Smith elected by a landslide.

December   In New York City for the winter and resumed regular
                    visits to his office.

1923

During the year drew up a plan to preserve world peace for "The American Peace Award," offered by Edward Bok. Mrs. Roosevelt was named to the Jury of Award, and the plan was not submitted for award, probably for that reason. The plan is reprinted in full in This I Remember by Eleanor Roosevelt.

Feb. - March   Cruised in the Florida Keys. Continued practice for next three years.

July   Appealed for understanding and better relations with Japan in article in Asia.

November   Played active role in establishment of the Walter Hines Page School of International Relations at Johns Hopkins.

1924

May 1   Assumed management of Al Smith's campaign to secure the Democratic Presidential nomination.

June 26   On crutches in New York's Madison Square Garden, delivered nominating speech for Smith, calling him the "Happy Warrior" of the political battlefield.

July 8   Addressed convention in attempt to break a deadlock between Smith and William Gibbs McAdoo. A compromise candidate, John W. Davis, was finally selected on the one hundred and third ballot.

October 3   First visit to Warm Springs, Georgia, for mineral baths.

December   Addressed a circular letter to the rank and file of the Democratic Party of the nation asking advice on what policies the Party should adopt, but also stating his own views. Received many replies.

December   Ended law partnership with Marvin and Emmet, too old-fashioned for his tastes, and entered into a new one with D. Basil O'Connor. Kept interest in business, engaging in various speculative enterprises during the next few years.

1925

February 28   Proposed a conference of leading Democrats to try to end the factional character of the Party and find a new ideologocal (progressive, he hoped) consensus. Conservative Democrats, led by John W. Davis, blocked the move.

April 9   Appointed by Governor Smith to the Taconic State Park Commission and was elected chairman. In conflict with Robert Moses, president of New York State Council of Parks, over apportionment of funds for roads.

1926

May   Delivered commencement address at Milton Academy, an appeal to liberalism entitled "Whither Bound?" Published later in the year as a small book.

September 27   Delivered keynote speech at New York Democratic State Convention; resisted attempts to nominate him for United States Senator.

1927

Spent much of year attempting to counter the charges that Al Smith, as President, would be controlled by Tammany and the Catholic Church, as well as being a "wet."

February 1   Formed the Georgia Warm Springs Foundation, ultimately putting two hundred thousand dollars into it, over two-thirds of his wealth. Built cottage there and bought a large farm nearby.

1928

June 17   At Democratic National Convention in Houston, Texas nominated Al Smith for President. Effectively used the radio to project himself as well as Smith.

July   Wrote article on Democratic foreign policy for Foreign Affairs.

September   Strong pressure was exerted by Democratic leaders in New York to get Roosevelt to run for governor. He constantly refused, pleading health and his investment at Warm Springs.

October 1   Gave in to final plea by Al Smith.

October 2   Nominated for governor by Mayor Jimmy Walker of New York City.

October 16   Officially accepted nomination for governor.

October 17   Speech at Binghamton opened campaign. Samuel I. Rosenman joined staff and played increasingly important role in advising F.D.R.

November 3   Closed a strenuous campaign at Madison Square Garden in New York City.

November 6   Elected Governor of New York, defeating the Republican Albert Ottinger by the narrow margin of 25,564 votes out of four and a quarter million. Herbert Lehman elected Lieutenant Governor. Although Smith lost the presidency to Hoover, the Democrats made significant gains in the cities.

December 29   Resigned as Commissioner (and Chairman) of the Taconic State Park Commission.

GOVERNOR AND PRESIDENTIAL CANDIDATE

1929

January 1   Inaugurated Governor of New York. Kept most of outgoing Governor Smith's department heads, but rankled Smith by replacing Secretary of State Robert Moses with Edward J. Flynn; Industrial Commissioner Dr. James A. Hamilton with Miss Frances Perkins, and especially when he failed to reappoint Belle Moskowitz as his secretary.

January 3   Appointed an Agricultural Advisory Commission with
               Henry Morgenthau, Jr., of Hopewell Junction in Dutch-
               ess County as Chairman. Morganthau was the pub-
               lisher of the American Agriculturist.

March 12   Proposed plan for developing the water power resources
               of the St. Lawrence River.

April   Battled with legislature over the budget. Eventually
               (November) his position sustained by the courts.

May 15   Appointed Samuel I. Rosenman as Counsel to the Gov-
               ernor.

June   Awarded honorary degrees by Harvard, Hobart, Dart-
               mouth and Fordham. Eventually received thirty such
               degrees. Mrs. Roosevelt received thirty-four.

October   Refused to make an investigation of municipal corrup-
               tion in New York City until definite facts were alleged.
               Mayor James J. Walker was being opposed by Repre-
               sentative Fiorello La Guardia. Walker's victory in
               November did not end the charges, and Walker finally
               resigned on September 1, 1932 with a bitter attack on
               Roosevelt.

                              1930
April 10   Signed Old-Age Assistance bill for New York State.

April 26   Attacked concentration of wealth in Jefferson Day ad-
               dress to the National Democratic Club in New York
               City. Was touted for national leadership by Senator
               Burton K. Wheeler of Montana.

June 30   Attacked Hoover policies in speech at Governor's Con-
               ference in Salt Lake City, Utah. Roosevelt asked for
               conservatism in spending.

September 9   Advocated repeal of the Eighteenth Amendment, re-
               placing it with state controls and local options.

October 18-30   Toured state giving campaign speeches in major cities.
                  His evident stamina was amazing, considering his al-
                  most useless legs.

November 1   Final campaign speech at Carnegie Hall in New York
                  City.

November 4   Reelected Governor over the Republican Charles H.
                  Tuttle with a majority of over 700,000 votes, even car-
                  rying upstate New York. Shortly thereafter, Roosevelt,
                  with Flynn and Howe concurring, decided that in view
                  of this landslide vote, 1932 was the year to try for the
                  Presidency.

December 11   A leading New York bank, the Bank of the United States,
                  failed. Roosevelt called for banking reform to protect
                  depositors.

                                    1931
January   Hose set up "Friends of Roosevelt" organization in
                  New York City.

                  James A. Farley selected to manage the campaign to
                  elect Roosevelt the next president.

March 3   Hoover vetoed a Muscle Shoals bill, proposed by Senator
                  George W. Norris, to develop the Tennessee Valley.

March 5   An attempt by John J. Raskob and Al Smith to turn the
                  Democratic Party to a pro-wet, high-tariff position was
                  thwarted by Roosevelt strategy, devised by Howe, Flynn
                  and Farley, which courted Southern support of such
                  leaders as Cordell Hull.

Mar. 29-April 17 Polls of leading Democrats indicated Roosevelt was the
                  favorite candidate for president of more than half of
                  those polled.

April 20   Approved bill regulating hours of labor for women and
                  children in New York State.

May 1   Gave address at opening of the Empire State building.

June 2   Challenged governors of the states at French Lick, Indiana to apply new remedies and positive leadership in attempting to solve problems.

June 21   Hoover proposed a one year "moratorium" on reparations and war debts.

July 25   Medical report on Roosevelt's health appearing in Liberty magazine gave him a highly favorable assessment.

August 15   Called special session of state legislature to consider problems of unemployment and relief. Called for a Temporary Emergency Relief Administration to provide public works, paid for by additional taxation. The agency, created the following month, was a model for other states and for the later New Deal agencies like it, (T.E.R.A.) alphabetically labelled.

August 28   Recommended creation of a Relief Administration for the unemployed at special session of the State Legislature. $20,000,000 appropriated; the first effective state action to relieve unemployment distress. This (Wicks Bill) created a Temporary Emergency Relief Administration headed by Jesse I. Straus, of R.H. Macy, as chairman and with Harry L. Hopkins its executive director. Hopkins succeeded Straus at the latter's resignation in 1932.

September 18   Japan invaded Manchuria, the first violation of the Kellog-Briand Pact and the beginning of the events which led to World War II.

Oct. - Nov.   Al Smith opposed bond issue for reforestation in New York. Roosevelt favored it in letters and speeches and eventually saw its acceptance by the voters.

October 24   Gave address at opening of the George Washington Bridge.

December 2   Al Smith revealed his animosity toward Roosevelt (for,
                  among other things, failure to seek his advice) to Clark
                  Howell, publisher of the <u>Atlanta Constitution</u>. Howell
                  promptly reported the conversation to Roosevelt.

                                    1932
January 1   William Randolph Hearst launched attack against "in-
                  ternationalists" like Roosevelt and others who followed
                  the policies of Woodrow Wilson. His papers came out
                  in support of John Nance Garner.

January 8   Walter Lippmann's column in the New York <u>World</u> ac-
                  cused Roosevelt of "two-faced platitudes" and a lack of
                  any real convictions -- "a pleasant man who, without
                  any important qualifications for the office, would very
                  much like to be President."

January 22   President Hoover signed the bill creating the Recon-
                  struction Finance Corporation, capitalized at $500 mil-
                  lion and authorized to borrow up to $2 billion to pro-
                  vide loans for banks, life insurance companies, rail-
                  roads, and farm mortgage and building and loan asso-
                  ciations. On July 21, the act was broadened to include
                  additional loans, as well as loans to states and munici-
                  palities for public works.

January 23   Authorized entrance of his name in North Dakota pri-
                  mary, thus formally announcing his candidacy for the
                  Democratic nomination for President.

February 2   Roosevelt, addressing the New York State Grange, de-
                  clared that he did not now favor American participation
                  in the League of Nations.

February 6   Al Smith announced that he would be available for the
                  nomination if it were offered to him.

February 27   The Glass-Steagall Act was signed, providing $750 mil-
                  lion for business loans to be created by allowing com-
                  mercial paper to meet the rediscount policy of the Fed-
                  eral Reserve System.

March   Rosenman, aided by Professor Raymond Moley of Bar-
               nard, assembled a "brains trust," including Rexford
               Guy Tugwell (economics), Adolph A. Berle, Jr. (eco-
               nomics), D. Basil ("Doc") O'Connor, Roosevelt's law
               partner and many others. The term, later shortened
               to "Brain Trust," was first used by James M. Kieran
               of the New York Times. Roosevelt himself liked to
               call it his "Privy Council."

March 2   Made final effort to obtain adequate legislation to regu-
               late public utility companies.

March 17   Signed four bills providing credit facilities for crop
               production.

April 8   Broadcast "forgotten man" speech, which demonstrated
               his political philosophy and attacked the so-called
               "trickle down" theory.

April 13   Al Smith, addressing leading Democrats in Washington,
               challenged Roosevelt by offering to "fight to the end --
               against any candidate who persists in any demagogic
               appeal to the masses of the working people of this coun-
               try to destroy themselves by setting class against class
               and rich against poor."

May 22   Speech at Oglethorpe University called for progressive
               policies and bold experiments.

May 29-July 29 "Bonus Army" of about 2,000 veterans and their families
               camped on Anacostia Flats in Washington, D.C. de-
               manding cash payment of their compensation certifi-
               cates. Federal troops, on order of President Hoover
               and commanded by General Douglas A. MacArthur, dis-
               persed them with machine guns, bayonets, tanks, and
               tear gas.

June 14-16   Republican National Convention at Chicago renominated
               Herbert Hoover and Charles Curtis on first ballot.

June 27-July 2   Democratic National Convention met in Chicago. Anti-Roosevelt forces, led by Al Smith, blocked an attempt to change the two-thirds rule.

June 30   The Democratic platform called for a balanced budget, with drastic cuts in government spending. It advocated banking and investment reforms, state unemployment and old-age insurance, farm price supports, and the repeal of Prohibition.

July 1   Nominated for President on the fourth ballot. Release of the Texas and California delegations by John Nance Garner, Speaker of the House of Representatives, swung the tide. A reported deal with Hearst was believed to have swung Garner to support Roosevelt and the California switch was announced by William G. McAdoo, a close Hearst friend.

July 2   Broke tradition by flying to Chicago to accept the nomination and address the convention. His speech included a pledge for "a new deal for the American people." This phrase, while not new, stuck.

Garner nominated for Vice President.

July 11   Hoover vetoed the Garner-Wagner relief bill which would have provided direct Federal relief aid and vast public works.

July 22   A Federal Home Loan Bank Act was signed by Hoover to decrease mortgage foreclosures and to encourage home construction.

Aug. - Oct.   Campaigned throughout country. No clear cut philosophy emerged, with contradictory positions on government spending and the need for aid to the unemployed. Some indications of the New Deal did appear, with a stress on the need for government regulation of Wall Street, planning, government-business cooperation, and welfare over budget balancing.

September 1   After a hearing before the Governor in Albany and before he was dismissed as Mayor of New York for improper use of his office, Jimmy Walker resigned and fled to Europe. Roosevelt had stood up to Tammany and a bothersome issue was removed.

September 23   A particularly important campaign speech, delivered at the Commonwealth Club in San Francisco, stated his political philosophy.

September 29   Tammany showed its anti-Roosevelt attitude by rejecting Justice Samuel I. Rosenman for a full-term nomination to the State Supreme Court. Roosevelt had given Rosenman an interim appointment.

November 8   Elected President, with 22,821,857 votes to Hoover's 15,761,845. Norman Thomas, Socialist Party, received 881,951 and William Z. Foster, Communist Party, received 102,785. The electoral vote was 472 to 50, Roosevelt carrying 42 of the 48 states.

November 22   Met with Hoover at White House in attempt by Hoover to attain a common position on war debts. The meeting was useless, with Roosevelt refusing to be bound by an international agreement on the gold standard.

                                1933
January 2   Gave address at the inauguration of his successor for governor, Herbert H. Lehman.

January   While vacationing in Warm Springs met Senator Norris at Muscle Shoals and discussed his vision of a multi-use development of the Tennessee River.

January 9   Met with Secretary of State Henry L. Stimson at Hyde Park on invitation from the President-elect. Discussed foreign policy matters at length.

February 6   Twentieth Amendment to the Constitution declared ratified. This so-called "lame duck" amendment would move future inaugurations from March 4 to January 20 and the opening of Congress to January 3.

February 14 Bank failures in Michigan led to a "bank holiday," closing all banks in state. (Earlier "holidays" had been
declared in Nevada, October 31, 1932 and in Lousiana
by Governor Huey Long on February 4, 1933). Succes-
sive runs on banks by depositors in other states led to
bank holidays, finally culminating in the closing of
banks in New York by Governor Herbert H. Lehman on
Inauguration Day.

February 15 Assassination attempt on Roosevelt at Miami, Florida
by bricklayer Giuseppe Zangara, shouting "too many
people are starving to death." Mayor Anton J. Cermak
of Chicago was mortally wounded, dying March 6. Zangara was executed two weeks later.

February 17 Hoover appealed to Roosevelt to restore confidence by
promising to balance the budget and maintain a sound
currency upon taking office. Roosevelt all but ignored
the request.

March 3 Hoover refused to declare a nation-wide bank holiday
as advised by the Federal Reserve Board.

FIRST TERM

1933

March 4 Inaugurated. Called for the use of "broad Executive
power" and stated that "the only thing we have to fear
is fear itself." Used term "good neighbor" for foreign
policy.

Cabinet members (all sworn in on this day): Cordell
Hull of Tennessee, Secretary of State; William H.
Woodin of New York, Secretary of the Treasury; George
H. Dern of Utah, Secretary of War; Homer S. Cummings
of Connecticut, Attorney General; James A. Farley of
New York, Postmaster General; Claude A. Swanson of
Virginia, Secretary of the Navy; Harold L. Ickes of

Illinois, Secretary of the Interior; Henry A. Wallace of Iowa, Secretary of Agriculture; Daniel C. Roper of South Carolina, Secretary of Commerce; and Frances Perkins of New York, Secretary of Labor.

March 5   Called a special session of Congress to meet March 9. Declared a four day bank holiday, suspending all financial transactions, government as well as private.

March 6   Appointed: William Phillips, Under Secretary of State; Raymond Moley, Assistant Secretary of State; Rexford G. Tugwell, Assistant Secretary of Agriculture; Lewis W. Douglas, Director of the Budget; Henry Morgenthau, Jr., Director of the Federal Farm Board; Stephen Early and Marvin H. McIntyre, Presidential Aides. Other key appointments were Colonel Edwin M. (Pa) Watson as military aide, Rudolph Forster to continue as executive clerk, and Grace Tully to assist Marguerite (Missy) Le Hand as his personal secretary.

March 8   Held first press conference as President, the total for his four terms to reach almost a thousand. Many of his remarks were preceded by "off the record...."

HUNDRED DAYS

March 9   Emergency Banking Relief Act, introduced, passed and signed the same day, put banks under federal (Presidential) control and provided for their re-opening.

March 10   Proposed cuts in salaries of government employees and other reductions in government spending totaling $500 million.

March 12   Gave first "fireside chat," addressing America by radio with an audience estimated at sixty million people.

March 13   Appointed Jesse Straus ambassador to France; Robert
                Bingham, ambassador to Great Britain; Josephus Daniels
                ambassador to Mexico.

                Asked Congress for an early end to Prohibition.

March 16   Sent message on agricultural problems to Congress.

March 20   Signed the Economy Act, proposed on March 10, and
                passed by the House on March 11 and the Senate on
                March 15. The actual saving proved to be about $243
                million.

March 21   Asked Congress for three measures to combat unem-
                ployment, a Civilian Conservation Corps (CCC), a re-
                lief program for states (eventually FERA), and a pro-
                gram for industrial stimulation (eventually NIRA).

March 22   Signed the Beer-Wine Revenue Act, legalizing 3.2 per
                cent beer and 4 per cent wine.

March 23   Reappointed Joseph C. Grew as ambassador to Japan.

March 27   Issued Executive Order consolidating several Federal
                agencies involving farmers, into one, the Farm Credit
                Administration (FCA).

March 29   Sent Congress recommendations for federal regulation
                of securities. Ferdinand Pecora, counsel of the Senate
                Banking and Currency Committee, had been conducting
                an investigation since late 1932 and had put leading fi-
                nanciers on the witness stand, among them J.P. Morgan.

March 31   Signed bill establishing the Civilian Conservation Corps
                (CCC), to create employment for young men and to aid
                in reforestation work.

April 3   Appointed Claude G. Bowers as ambassador to Spain;
                Sumner Welles, Assistant Secretary of State. Welles
                appointed ambassador to Cuba on April 21 to try to
                mediate between opposing groups.

April 4   Proposed conference of world leaders to meet in Wash-
                 ington.

April 10   Requested that Congress create a Tennessee Valley
                 Authority.

April 12   Appointed Ruth Bryan Owens, the daughter of William
                 Jennings Bryan, minister to Denmark. This was the
                 first woman to represent the United States as a minister
                 abroad.

April 15   Appointed John Collier, Sr., as Commissioner of Indian
                 Affairs.

April 16   Signed the Johnson-O'Malley Act providing federal aid
                 to states for Indian welfare.

April 19   Announced that the United States was off the gold stand-
                 ard, thus freeing him to practice various measures to
                 raise domestic prices.

April 20   Appointed Breckenridge Long ambassador to Italy.

April 23   Met with Prime Minister J. Ramsay MacDonald of Great
                 Britain on the yacht Sequoia on the Potomac. Discussed
                 disarmament and economic affairs.

April 24   Conferred with Premier Edouard Herriot of France in
                 Washington.

May 3   Appointed Dean G. Acheson Under Secretary of the
                 Treasury. Confirmed, after a struggle in the Senate,
                 on May 17.

May 5   Jesse Jones, appointed to the board of the Reconstruc-
                 tion Finance Corporation (RFC) by Hoover in 1932, was
                 elected chairman. Jones also served (1933-1939) on
                 the National Emergency Council.

May 12   Signed act creating the Federal Emergency Relief Administration (FERA) to aid states in relief problems. Appointed Harry L. Hopkins its Administrator May 19.

Signed the Agricultural Adjustment Act, designed to restore the purchasing power of farmers by establishing parity prices on certain commodities. The Administration it created (AAA) was to be financed by a processing tax on manufacturers. The bill also authorized the President to devalue the gold content of the dollar up to 50 per cent. Appointed George N. Peek administrator.

May 15   Appointed Secretary of State Hull, James M. Cox, of Ohio and Senator Kay Pittman of Nevada as delegates to the World Economic Conference in London. Other delegates appointed were Senator James Couzens of Michigan, Representative Samuel D. McReynolds of Tennessee, and Ralph W. Morrison of Texas.

May 16   Addressed an appeal to 52 heads of states appealing for success of the Disarmament Conference. The message was drafted in the fear that the recently elected Chancellor of Germany, Adolph Hitler, was planning to call for German rearmament. Roosevelt backed down on concrete proposals when Senate isolationists threatened neutrality legislation to curb his power.

May 18   Signed the Tennessee Valley Authority Act, to reclaim and modernize the valley of the river in seven different states by building multi-purpose dams. The project was also designed as a "yardstick" for charges levied by private utilities.

May 19   Appointed Arthur E. Morgan chairman of the Tennessee Valley Authority (TVA), with David E. Lilienthal and Harcourt Morgan the other directors.

May 23   Appointed J. P. Warburg and Herbert Feis to head technical staff at the London Economic Conference.

May 27   Signed the Federal Securities Act, (Truth-in-securities Act) providing regulations to require full disclosure to investors on new securities.

June 5   A Joint Resolution of Congress repudiated the gold clause in all government and private contracts.

June 6   Signed the National Employment System Act establishing the United States Employment Service.

June 10   Appointed William Dodd ambassador to Germany.

June 12   The World Economic Conference in London opened. It was hoped that it might reduce tariffs, increase trade, and stabilize currencies.

June 13   Signed the Home Owners Refinancing Act creating the Home Owners Loan Corporation (HOLC) to aid in financing home mortgages.

June 16   Signed the Banking Act of 1933 (the Glass-Steagall Act) creating the Federal Bank Deposit Insurance Corporation (FDIC) to insure deposits up to $5,000. The bill also extended the operations of the Federal Reserve System.

                Signed the Farm Credit Act, refinancing farm mortgages on a low interest, long term basis.

                Signed the Emergency Railroad Transportation Act, consolidating railroad operations and creating the office of Federal Coordinator of Transportation, appointing Joseph B. Eastman to the post.

                Signed the National Industrial Recovery Act (NIRA) creating the National Recovery Administration (NRA) to supervise industry's attempt at self-regulation by establishing fair trade in competition codes. Section 7a of the act guaranteed labor's right to collective bargaining. The "Blue Eagle" became the sign of the cooperation.

General Hugh S. Johnson appointed NRA administrator on same day. Title II of the NIRA created the Public Works Administration (PWA) to provide $3.3 billion in public works and Secretary of the Interior Harold L. Ickes was named to head the agency on July 8.

Congress adjourned, ending the special session of the 73rd Congress and bringing to a close the eventful Hundred Days. Roosevelt had sent fifteen messages to Congress and had achieved fifteen important and historic laws.

REMAINDER OF FIRST TERM

June 27
Raymond Moley arrived in London, supposedly with instructions from Roosevelt for the World Economic Conference. Roosevelt pulled the rug out from under Moley in a message sent July 1, and finally in his message to Hull on July 2.

July 2
Had radiogram sent to Secretary Hull in London ordering him not to agree to go back on the gold standard. Made public in London the next day, this was the so-called "bombshell" message in which Roosevelt was accused of "torpedoing" the conference.

July 9
First industrial code under NRA approved, that of the cotton textile industry. Other important codes: oil, steel and lumber (August 19) and the automobile industry (August 27).

July 11
Created an Executive Council, to be made up of heads of departments and agencies. Ineffective, it was superceded by the National Emergency Council, then consolidated with it on October 29, 1934.

Secretary of State Hull, from London, complained to Roosevelt about Moley's lack of loyalty.

July 21	In press conference referred (off the record) to the London Conference as "the damn thing."
July 24	In a "fireside chat" explained the NIRA to the American people, and launched the Roll of Honor (Blue Eagle) campaign.
July 27	Hull sailed from Great Britain. The World Economic Conference was as good as "dead."
August 27	Raymond Moley resigned as Assistant Secretary of State to become editor of the national weekly, Today. Moley came to criticize the New Deal, especially in his After Seven Years, published in 1939.
September 7	Appointed Walter J. Cummings director of the Federal Deposit Insurance Corporation (FDIC). Cummings was elected chairman.
October 7	Dismissed William E. Humphrey, a Hoover appointee to the Federal Trade Commission, after Humphrey had refused to resign as the President had requested on July 25, and again on August 31. Humphrey's appointment was until 1938. The Supreme Court, on May 27, 1935, denied that the President had such power.
	Appointed James H. Landis as Federal Trade Commissioner.
October 17	Issued a declaration, jointly arrived at in Washington with President Harmodio Arias, giving Panama certain commercial rights in the Canal Zone.
October 18	Commodity Credit Corporation, acting under the AAA, authorized to loan RFC money to farmers on their crops, mostly cotton.
October 22	Announced the authorization by the RFC to establish a "commodity dollar" by manipulating the gold content of the dollar. Operations started on October 25.

November 8   Set up a Civil Works Administration (CWA) to admin-
                  ister an unemployment relief program, with funds from
                  FERA and PWA appropriations, as well as from local
                  governments. Harry L. Hopkins appointed Administra-
                  tor. Functions taken over by FERA in March, 1934.

November 13   Henry Morgenthau, Jr. designated Acting Secretary
                  of the Treasury because of the ill health of Secretary
                  William H. Woodin. Woodin died early in the next year.

November 15   Dean Acheson resigned as Under Secretary of the Treas-
                  ury. Acheson, as well as his chief assistants Oliver
                  Sprague and James Warburg, opposed Roosevelt's gold
                  buying scheme.

November 16   Recognized the Union of Soviet Socialist Republics.

November 18   William C. Bullitt appointed first ambassador to the
                  Soviet Union.

November 21   O.W.M. Sprague resigned advisory post in the Treas-
                  ury Department in protest against the President's pol-
                  icy of buying gold to try to bring up prices of goods.

November 25   Al Smith opposed Roosevelt's financial policy, saying
                  that he was for gold dollars as against "baloney dollars."

December 3-26   Montevideo Conference, attended by Secretary of State
                  Hull, renounced the right of intervention by any state
                  in the Americas in the internal or external affairs of
                  another.

December 5   Declared that the 21st Amendment had been ratified
                  when Utah became the 36th state to enact the amend-
                  ment. Thus the 18th (Prohibition) Amendment was re-
                  pealed.

December 11   George N. Peek made special advisor on foreign trade,
                  easing him out of the AAA where he was at odds with
                  the liberal faction, represented by Tugwell and Jerome
                  Frank.

December 19   Told Mrs. Roosevelt that "politically speaking" it would
                 be wise for her not to be involved with urging American
                 adherence to the World Court.

December 21   Ordered the Treasury to buy the annual output of silver
                 at 64.5 cents an ounce, 21.5 cents more than the cur-
                 rent market price.

December 31   John Maynard Keynes addressed an "open letter" to
                 Roosevelt in the New York Times advocating deficit
                 spending rather than reform.

                                    1934

January   Dr. Francis Townsend of Long Beach, California set
                 up the Old Age Revolving Pension plan - 200 dollars a
                 month to every person over 60, all to be spent in a
                 month - financed by a 2 per cent tax on all business
                 transactions. The idea intrigued millions of supporters.

January 1   Henry Morgenthau, Jr. of New York appointed as Sec-
                 retary of the Treasury.

January 3   In first Annual Message to the Seventy-third Congress
                 in its first regular session, praised Congress for its
                 efforts to curb exploitation of people and resources.
                 Denounced lynching and other crimes.

January 4   Received the budget for the last half of the fiscal year
                 calling for expenditures of $10 billion with a deficit of
                 $7 billion.

January 8   Alexander A. Troyanovsky accredited first ambassador
                 from the U.S.S.R.

January 15   Special message to Congress asked that the dollar be
                 stabilized between 50 and 60 per cent of the gold dollar.

January 26   Huey Long, the Louisiana "Kingfish" formed the "Share
                 Our Wealth" organization, with programs far to the left
                 of Roosevelt's New Deal. Gerald L.K. Smith, a Shreve-
                 port, Louisiana minister, became a national organizer.

January 30   Signed the Gold Reserve Act, giving him the power to set the valuation of the dollar at 50 to 60 per cent of it's original gold content. Called it "the nicest birthday present I ever had."

January 31   Proclaimed the gold valuation of the dollar to be 59.06 cents.

Signed the Farm Mortgage Refinancing Act establishing the Federal Farm Mortgage Corporation (FFMC) to aid in financing farm mortgages.

February 2   Established an Export-Import Bank to stimulate trade with other nations. A subsidiary of RFC, it was under the direction of RFC Administrator Jesse Jones.

Appointed Leo T. Crowley director of the Federal Deposit Insurance Corporation to succeed Walter J. Cummings, retiring.

February 9   Special message to Congress asked that it regulate stock exchange transactions.

February 15   Signed the Civil Works Emergency Relief Act providing funds for civil works under FERA. The program became the Works Progress Administration (WPA) in April, 1935.

February 19   Ordered Postmaster General Farley to cancel all domestic air mail contracts, charging collusion.

February 23   Signed the Crop Loan Act providing $40 million for farmers.

March 2   Asked Congress for authority to negotiate tariff agreements on a reciprocal basis. Secretary of State Cordell Hull strongly favored such "free-trade" actions.

March 7   Created a review board to study monopolistic tendencies of the NRA codes. Noted lawyer Clarence Darrow appointed to direct the investigation.

March 14   At press conference, asked to comment on the impending defeat of the St. Lawrence Treaty (the Senate failed to ratify it that same day), said, "the thing is going through; perhaps not today, but the St. Lawrence Seaway is going to be built just as sure as God made little apples." The prediction came true twenty years later.

March 24   Signed the Tydings-McDuffie Act, providing independence for the Philippines. Approved a constitution for the new country on February 8, 1935. Independence became official on July 4, 1946.

March 27   Signed the Vinson Naval Parity Act, authorizing the building of the navy up to the limitations set by the Washington Naval Limitation Treaty (1922) and the London Treaty (1930). Congress failed to provide sufficient funds to meet the construction needs.

Vetoed an Independent Offices Act which was aimed at restoring salaries of government employees cut by the Economy Act of 1933. The House (March 27) and Senate (March 28) overrode his veto.

Roosevelt vetoed a total of 633 bills, mostly "relief" or pension types. 9 vetoes were overridden. His veto total, of course for more terms, was the greatest of all presidents, even exceeding Grover Cleveland's of 413.

Mar. 28-April 12 On fishing trip in West Indies on the yacht Nourmahal.

April 7   Signed the Jones-Connally Farm Relief Act, adding other commodities such as barley, rye, peanuts and cattle to the list enumerated under AAA.

April 13   Signed the Johnson Debt Default Act, forbidding loans
                  to any nation not paying its debt to the United States.

April 21   Signed the Cotton Control Act (Bankhead Act) requiring
                  compulsory reduction of cotton growing over the set
                  quota.

April 23   Senator Gerald P. Nye of North Dakota became chair-
                  man of a Senate Munitions Investigating Committee to
                  inquire into the manufacture and sale of arms. The
                  Nye Committee, a key factor in isolationist sentiment,
                  continued until 1936.

April 24   Appointed Rexford G. Tugwell Under Secretary of
                  Agriculture.

April 27   Signed the Home Owners Loan Act, which guaranteed
                  up to $2 billion on home mortgages under HOLC.

April 28   Urged Congress to pass an Indian Reorganization Bill
                  (Wheeler-Howard) and restore Indian culture.

April 30   Signed a bill to protect Indians from claims made by
                  defaulting purchasers of Indian heirship lands.

May 9   Signed the Jones-Costigan Sugar Act adding beet and cane
                  sugar to the AAA list of quota commodities. Cuban
                  sugar imports were also included.

May 18   Signed the Crime Control Acts, six laws designed to
                  combat rising gangsterism, and especially kidnapping -
                  the last a result of the abduction and murder of the in-
                  fant son of Charles A. and Anne Morow Lindbergh in
                  1932.

May 21   Signed bill repealing 12 sections of obsolete Indian laws.

May 24   Signed the Municipal Bankruptcy Act, easing the debt
                  structure of local governments.

May 28   Met with John Maynard Keynes, with Keynes dismayed by Roosevelt's lack of knowledge in economics, and the President unimpressed with Keynes' knowledge of political reality.

May 29   Signed treaty with Cuba abrogating the Platt Amendment. Sumner Welles was chiefly responsible for the agreement.

              Appointed Harry L. Hopkins Federal Housing Administrator (FHA).

June 6   Signed Securities Exchange Act creating the Securities and Exchange Commission (SEC), with powers to regulate stock exchange practices. Benjamin V. Cohen and Thomas G. Corcoran wrote most of the law and were seen to be key figures in drafting New Deal legislation and selling it to Congress.

June 7   Signed the Corporate Bankruptcy Act, easing debt reorganization of corporations.

June 12   Signed the Reciprocal Trade Agreements Act, authorizing him to raise or lower tariffs up to 50 per cent with reciprocating countries.

              Signed the Farm Mortgage Foreclosure Act to aid farmers in regaining their property.

              Signed Air Mail Act giving the Interstate Commerce Commission power to set rates on air mail. Provided for a Federal Aviation Commission, with Clark Howell appointed as chairman (June 30).

June 15   Signed the National Guard Act, putting the Guard under the regular Army in time of war or national emergency declared by Congress.

              Finland paid in full its installment on its war debt, the only nation to do so.

June 16   Signed the Crime Prevention Compact Act, allowing
                   states to cooperate in the prevention of crime.

June 18   Signed the Indian Reorganization Act (Wheeler-Howard)
                   ending the allotment system of the Dawes Severalty Act
                   of 1887 and restoring lands to common ownership.
                   Tribes were encouraged to draw up their own constitu-
                   tions.

June 19   Signed the Communications Act establishing the Federal
                   Communications Commission (FCC) to regulate inter-
                   state and foreign communication by telegraph, cable,
                   and radio.

                   Signed the Silver Purchase Act, directing the Secretary
                   of the Treasury to buy silver until it reached one-fourth
                   of the nation's reserve, or until the world price reached
                   1.29 dollars an ounce. Roosevelt had had to yield to
                   the silver bloc.

                   By a resolution of Congress was empowered to establish
                   a National Labor Relations Board (NLRB) to replace the
                   1933 National Labor Board. Senator Robert Wagner of
                   New York, unpopular with business leaders, was by-
                   passed by Roosevelt in appointing the new board.

June 22   Appointed Frank R. McNinch chairman of the Federal
                   Power Commission.

June 27   The Railroad Retirement Act of 1934 was declared un-
                   constitutional by the Supreme Court in Railroad Retire-
                   ment Board v. Alton R. R. Company.

                   Signed the Railway Labor Act (Crosser-Dill) giving
                   workers the right to bargain collectively and setting up
                   a mediation board to handle disputes.

June 28   Signed the Federal Farm Bankruptcy Act (Frazier-
                   Lemke) providing a five year moratorium on foreclo-
                   sures. Declared unconstitutional in 1935, was replaced
                   by a second Frazier-Lemke Act on August 29, 1935.

Signed the National Housing Act to encourage home construction and setting up the Federal Housing Administration (FHA) to insure loans. James A. Moffet of New York appointed to head agency on June 30.

Signed the Tobacco Control Act (Kerr-Smith), adding tobacco to the cumpulsory quota list.

Signed the Taylor Grazing Act, setting aside up to eight million acres of public grasslands.

June 29   Declared an embargo on the shipment of arms and munitions to Cuba except under license from the State Department.

June 30   Appointed Joseph P. Kennedy member of the Securities and Exchange Commission. Kennedy, father of the future president, John F. Kennedy, was elected chairman on July 2.

Appointed a National Labor Relations Board headed by Lloyd Garrison to replace the National Labor Board.

July 2-Aug. 9   Cruised to Hawaii through the Panama Canal on the U.S.S. Houston.

July 16   Violent strike in San Francisco harbor; Roosevelt refused to intervene. Strikes during 1934 plagued almost the entire country, from taxi drivers in New York and Philadelphia to farm workers in California.

August 6   Ordered all United States troops to be withdrawn from Haiti by August 15.

August 15   United States marines left Haiti after an occupation of 19 years.

August 22   The (American) Liberty League was formed "to fight radicalism and defend property rights." Supported by many prominent business men (and Al Smith), it opposed the New Deal and Roosevelt.

August 28   Upton Sinclair, running on a radical, left of New Deal
                   (End Poverty in California) program, received the Dem-
                   ocratic nomination for Governor of California. Roose-
                   velt failed to support him and he lost in the November
                   election.

August 30   Budget director Lewis W. Douglas resigned, greatly
                   disturbed by Roosevelt's fiscal policies. Wrote the
                   highly critical The Liberal Tradition in 1935.

September 25   General Hugh Johnson resigned as NRA Administrator,
                   replaced by a five man NIRA board; actual control went
                   to NRA counsel Donald R. Richberg.

September 30   In fireside chat asked for end of monopolistic features
                   of NRA codes.

October 4   Appointed Norman H. Davis and Admiral William H.
                   Standley delegates to preliminary discussions in London
                   on renewal of the naval treaty with Great Britain.

October 29   Created a National Emergency Council composed of
                   Cabinet members and NRA administrators and headed
                   by Donald R. Richberg.

November 6   Congressional elections gave Democrats a gain of ten
                   seats in both houses. Harry S Truman of Missouri
                   was one of the new Democratic senators. The gain,
                   unusual in an off-year election, was a victory for
                   Roosevelt.

November 10   Appointed Marriner S. Eccles Governor of the Federal
                   Reserve Board to succeed Eugene R. Black.

November 11   The Reverend Charles Coughlin of Royal Oak, Michi-
                   gan, formed the National Union for Social Justice. At
                   first pro-Roosevelt, Father Coughlin moved increas-
                   ingly to the left, denouncing the NRA, the AAA, and
                   finally in 1936 labelling Roosevelt a "Great betrayer
                   and liar."

December 12   Reappointed General Douglas A. MacArthur as Chief of Staff. First appointed to post by President Hoover in 1930.

1935

January 4   Gave annual message to Congress which had convened the day before, first under the 20th amendment. Called for social reform, with programs to provide jobs, security against old age and illness - the emphasis to be on aid to workers and farmers. Some historians call this a "second New Deal."

January 7   Supreme Court decided in Panama Refining Co. and Amazon Petroleum Corp. v. Ryan that NIRA gave too much power to the President.

January 10   Representative Louis Ludlow of Indiana first introduced a resolution in the House proposing a constitutional amendment to make a declaration of war (except on invasion) contingent on a national referendum.

January 16   Sent message to the Senate assuring it that joining the World Court would in no way diminish or jeopardize the sovereignty of the United States. The Senate voted on adherence on January 29, 52 to 36, seven votes short of the necessary two-thirds. The President had not greatly exerted himself, and no further effort was made.

March 9   Told Breckenridge Long, Ambassador to Italy, (who had predicted A European war in two years) that "We, too, are going through a bad case of Huey Long and Father Coughlin influenza - the whole country aching in every bone."

March 22   Approved the Filipino Constitution developed as a result of the McDuffie-Tydings Bill of March 24, 1934, providing independence for the Philippines in the future.

April 8   Signed the Emergency Relief Appropriation Act, five
                 billion dollars for establishing a large scale federal
                 public works program through the Works Progress Ad-
                 ministration (WPA) under Harry L. Hopkins (appointed
                 May 7). WPA established several imaginative projects,
                 among them the Federal Theater Project, the Federal
                 Art Project, the Federal Writers' Project and the Na-
                 tional Youth Administration (NYA). Highly criticized
                 for waste and inefficiency, WPA spent 11 billion dollars
                 until terminated in 1943, providing millions of jobs and
                 constructing thousands of highways, buildings, parks
                 and artistic projects.

April 27   Signed the Soil Conservation Act, establishing a special
                 branch of the Agriculture Department for soil conser-
                 vation. Placed under Hugh H. Bennett, who had headed
                 the Soil Erosion Service of the Interior Department
                 since October, 1933.

May   Gave only weak support for a federal antilynching bill
                 (Wagner-Costigan) and it was killed in the Senate Judi-
                 ciary Committee. Apparently unwilling to take on the
                 Southerners he needed to put through his program, the
                 fight for civil rights for Negroes was largely fought
                 by Mrs. Roosevelt.

May 1   By Executive Order created the Resettlement Adminis-
                 tration (RA) to improve the lot of farm families not
                 aided by the AAA. Rexford G. Tugwell became its ad-
                 ministrator. RA built "green belt" towns, suburban
                 communities, outside Washington, Cincinnati, and Mil-
                 waukee.

May 11   The Rural Electrification Administration (REA) was
                 created under RA to bring electricity to rural areas.

May 22   Vetoed the Soldiers' Bonus Bill (Patman Bill), establish-
                 ing a precedent by delivering the veto message before
                 a joint session of Congress. The House overrode the
                 veto, but the Senate sustained it. A similar bill was
                 passed over his veto in January, 1936.

May 27   The Supreme Court in a 9-0 decision declared the NRA
                    unconstitutional. The case involved the Live Poultry
                    Code of the NRA, and is often called the "sick chicken"
                    case, actually Schechter Poultry Corporation v. U.S.
                    Two other cases were decided against the New Deal.

June 19   Sent special message to Congress asking for increased
                    inheritance and income taxes.

June 26   By Executive Order established the National Youth Ad-
                    ministration (NYA) to give part time jobs to aid young
                    people in schools and colleges. Under WPA, the NYA
                    was placed under the direction of Aubrey Williams.

July 5   Signed the National Labor Relations Act (Wagner-Con-
                    nery) to replace section 7a of the NIRA, when that act
                    was declared unconstitutional. Roosevelt originally
                    opposed the measure, but changed his mind in May and
                    called it a "must." The bill, which guaranteed the right
                    of labor to join labor unions and to bargain collectively,
                    was upheld by the Supreme Court in March, 1937.

August 9   Signed the Motor Carrier Act placing buses and trucks
                    engaged in interstate commerce under the authority of
                    the Interstate Commerce Commission with power to
                    regulate rates.

August 14   Signed the Social Security Act, creating a federal sys-
                    tem of old-age and survivors' insurance, financed by
                    equal taxes from employer and employee (1 per cent in
                    1936). The law also provided for a federal-state plan
                    of unemployment insurance, as well as provisions for
                    dependent mothers and the crippled and blind.

August 23   Signed the Banking Act, revising the Federal Reserve
                    System as set up in 1913. The act increased federal
                    power over the banking system.

                    Appointed a new NLRB with Joseph W. Madden chairman.

	Appointed a Social Security Board with John G. Winant as chairman.
August 24	Signed bill amending the AAA to conform with the Supreme Court's decisions.
August 27	Signed act establishing the Indian Arts and Crafts Board, to encourage and protect Indian arts and crafts.
August 28	Signed the Public Utility Holding Company Act (Wheeler-Rayburn) preventing a public utility company from owning more than one utility.
August 30	Signed the Guffey-Snyder Bituminous Coal Stabilization Act, attempting to stabilize the soft coal industry by placing it under an NRA code. Replaced by the Guffey-Vinson Act in 1937 when declared unconstitutional by the Supreme Court.
	Signed the Revenue Act (or Wealth Tax Act) increasing the taxes on high incomes and excessive corporation profits. The surtax was raised to 75 per cent, and estate and gift taxes were increased.
August 31	Signed Neutrality Act of 1935, the first of several which attempted to keep the United States out of war. It forbade United States citizens from traveling on billigerent vessels except at their own risk, and prohibited the export of arms and munitions to belligerents. Roosevelt opposed the measure but signed it anyhow, after its effect was limited to 6 months.
September 6	Appointed Stewart McDonald as FHA administrator to succeed James A. Moffet.
September 8	Senator Huey P. Long was assassinated at Baton Rouge, Louisiana.
Sept. 26-Oct. 24	Train trip to California, dedicating Boulder (Hoover) Dam en route (September 30). Returned on U.S.S. Houston, through Panama Canal, fishing.

October 3   Proclaimed existence of a state of war between Italy and Ethiopia and imposed an arms embargo.

October 30   Agreed with Secretary of State Hull, in a dispute about trading with warring nations with Secretary of Commerce Roper, to keep the United States free of "those entanglements that move us along the road to war."

November 9   Committee for Industrial Organization (CIO) formed under A.F. of L.

November 14   Issued proclamation certifying the freedom of the Philippines and its elected officials. Manuel Quezon inaugurated as first President.

Signed reciprocal trade agreement with Canada.

November 15   Secretary Hull, with the approval of the President, warned against shipments of war supplies to Italy.

November 29   In Atlanta, Georgia, told an audience that the depth of the depression had passed and therefore the peak of federal spending.

December 23   Ordered the dissolution of NRA on January 1, 1936.

1936

January 3   In annual message warned of aggressive nations in the world, and of "fear mongers" at home menacing the New Deal.

January 6   The Supreme Court in a 6-3 vote declared the AAA unconstitutional in the U.S. v. Butler case.

January 16   Appointed William O. Douglas to the Securities and Exchange Commission (SEC). Douglas was immediately elected chairman.

January 24	Vetoed a Veterans' Bonus bill, but the bill, providing immediate payment of $1.5 billion in bonds to World War I veterans, was put into law on January 27 when both houses overrode the veto.
February 17	The TVA was upheld by the Supreme Court in Ashwander v. TVA.
February 29	Signed the Neutrality Act of 1936, extending the 1935 Act (August 31) until May 1, 1937. Signed a Soil Conservation and Domestic Allotment Act permitting the payment to farmers for land withdrawn for soil conservation purposes, thus rescuing some of his farm program after the Supreme Court had struck down the AAA.
March 2	Signed treaty with Panama modifying the Bunau-Varilly Treaty of 1903 and giving up the right of intervention. Not ratified by Senate until July 25, 1939 because of opposition of the military.
March 9	Hitler's invasion of the Rhineland brought letters to Roosevelt from his European ambassadors warning of an impending war. Roosevelt, watching closely, chose neutrality in word and action.
March 10	It was announced that Mrs. Roosevelt had traveled 115,000 miles in 3 years.
Mar. 23-April 8	Fishing trip on yacht Potomac in West Indies.
April 8	Louis Howe died.
May 18.	Supreme Court, in Carter v. Carter Coal Co., et al, declared the Guffey-Snyder Coal Conservation Act of 1935 unconstitutional because it violated the commerce clause.

June 1   Supreme Court, in Morehead v. Tipaldo reaffirmed the
                denial of a state the right to fix minimum wages for
                women and children. The 5-4 decision brought out the
                sharp division on the court on New Deal type legislation.
                Roosevelt the next day said that the majority on the
                court had created a "no-man's land."

June 9-12   The Republican Party's Convention met in Cleveland,
                Ohio, and on June 11, nominated Alfred M. Landon of
                Kansas for President and Frank Knox of Illinois for
                Vice President.

June 20   Signed the Federal Anti-Price Discrimination Act (Rob-
                inson-Patman) making it illegal to cut prices merely
                to undercut competition.

                Signed law exempting from taxation restricted Indian
                lands.

June 22   Signed the Revenue Act of 1936 which increased taxes
                on undistributed profits.

June 23-27   Roosevelt and Garner renominated by acclamation at
                the Democratic Party Convention in Philadelphia, Pa.
                Roosevelt was nominated on June 26, and in his accep-
                tance speech the next day attacked "economic royalists."

June 25   A low cost housing bill (Wagner-Ellenbogen) failed of
                passage in House. The bill had Roosevelt's only mild
                support.

June 26   Signed the Merchant Marine Act, creating the U.S.
                Maritime Commission.

June 30   Signed the Walsh-Healy Government Contracts Act to
                enforce payment of not less than minimum wages and
                a 40 hour week by contractors doing federal work.

                William Phillips succeeded Breckinridge Long as am-
                bassador to Italy.

July 14-28   Cruised to Nova Scotia on the schooner Senrinna.

August 14   Signed the Social Security Act, creating a federal sys-
                    tem of old-age and survivors' insurance. Appointed
                    John G. Winant of New Hampshire chairman August 23.

                    Told audience at Chautauqua, New York, "I hate war."

                    William Lemke of North Dakota nominated for Presi-
                    dent by the Union Party in Cleveland, Ohio. Thomas
                    C. O'Brien of Massachusetts was nominated for Vice
                    President. The party attracted followers of Father
                    Coughlin, Dr. Townsend, and Gerald L. K. Smith.

August 25   Appointed William C. Bullitt ambassador to France to
                    succeed Jesse Straus.

August 27   Secretary of War George H. Dern died. Harry H.
                    Woodring, Assistant Secretary, appointed to succeed
                    him on September 25.

September 18   Told Harvard audience, on celebration of its Tercen-
                    tenary, that Harvard and America should "stand for
                    the freedom of the human mind and carry the torch
                    of truth." Roosevelt had been rather silent during the
                    Hearst-inspired "red scare" in late 1934 and through-
                    out 1935.

October   Literary Digest polls predicted that Landon would de-
                    feat Roosevelt.

October 19   Ambassador to Germany William E. Dodd warned
                    Roosevelt that Hitler and Mussolini (who signed the
                    Rome-Berlin axis on October 25) meant to dominate
                    Europe and pled for United States cooperation with the
                    European democracies.

November 3   Reelected, receiving 27,476,673 votes to Landon's
                    16,679,583. William Lemke, Union Party, received
                    892,793; Norman Thomas, Socialist Party, received

187,720; Earl Browder, Communist Party, 80,159. Roosevelt received 523 of the 531 electoral votes, carrying all states except Maine and Vermont.

November 18   Sailed from Charlestown, South Carolina on the U.S.S. Indianapolis to attend Buenos Aires conference.

November 20   Joseph Davies confirmed as ambassador to the Soviet Union.

November 25   Told by French Ambassador William C. Bullitt that European democracies all felt "war is inevitable and Europe is doomed to destruction unless President Roosevelt intervenes." Hitler signed the anti-Comitern pact with Japan the next day. Italy joined on November 6, 1937.

November 27   Arrived at Rio de Janeiro, met by President Getulio Vargas of Brazil, and spoke before a joint session of Brazilian legislature.

November 30   Arrived at Buenos Aires and met President Agustin P. Justo of Argentina.

December 1   Addressed opening session of the Inter-American Conference. Secretary of State Hull and Under Secretary Welles also present. Returned home, arriving in Charlestown December 15.

December 23   The Buenos Aires Declaration pledged the 21 American states to consultation and non-intervention.

December 30   Sit-down strike by C.I.O. began at Flint, Michigan in General Motors Plant.

1937

January   Refused to intervene in sit-down strike although under pressure to do so.

January 1   Son James began service as assistant to the President.

January 6   Annual Message to Congress took Judicial branch to task for failing to meet the demands of democracy.

January 8   Put embargo on shipments of munitions to both sides in the Spanish Civil War. The war had begun the previous July. A joint resolution of Congress, January 6, extended the Neutrality Act to include civil wars.

January 12   Requested Congress to create six executive assistants to the president. Accomplished by Executive Order, September 8, 1939.

SECOND TERM

January 20   Inaugural Address listed the progress already made but still saw the need for social reform, with "one-third of a nation ill-housed, ill-clad, ill-nourished."

February 5   Proposed a bill to reorganize the Federal Judiciary, the Supreme Court to be increased (up to 15) by adding a member for every justice who did not retire at 70.

February 6   Former President Hoover and others attacked the "court packing" plan.

February 11 General Motors surrendered to the United Automobile Workers (C.I.O.) granting recognition as sole bargaining agent. Roosevelt had tacetly supported the sit-down tactics.

February 16 Sent special message to Congress asking aid for tenant farmers and sharecroppers.

March 1   Signed the Supreme Court Retirement Act, removing income tax hardships from justices who retired at 70.

March 4   Addressed Democratic Victory Dinners, in Washington and throughout nation, saying that only by making economic democracy work could elections continue to be won.

March 9   In "fireside chat" asked for support for his "court packing" bill. His aim was "to save the Constitution from the Court and the Court from itself."

March 29   Chief Justice Hughes and Associate Justice Roberts switched to the liberal view and, with Cardozo, Brandeis and Stone, handed down a 5-4 decision on minimum wages in West Coast Hotel Company v. Parrish.

April 12   Another 5-4 liberal decision by the Supreme Court upheld the National Labor Relations Act in National Labor Relations Board v. Jones and Laughlin Steel Corporation.

April 26   Signed the Guffey-Vinson Bituminous Coal Act setting up a code for the industry.

April 29-May 11   Fishing trip on U.S.S. Potomac in Gulf of Mexico.

May 1   Signed the Neutrality Act of 1937, giving the President power, whenever he proclaimed the existence of a state of war, to forbid Americans to sell arms and munitions to, loan money to, or travel on ships of, a belligerent nation. However a "cash and carry" clause was added, effective for two years.

May 6   Harry H. Woodring of Kansas, Acting Secretary of War, confirmed as Secretary of War.

Received word of Hindenburg disaster while on cruise.

May 19   Appointed Sumner Welles Under Secretary of State.

May 24   Sent special message to Congress asking that teeth be put into laws providing minimum wages and maximum hours. A Fair Labor Standards Act was passed in June, 1938.

The Supreme Court, 5-4, found the Social Security Act constitutional in Steward Machine Company v. Davis.

May 30

A Memorial Day "Massacre" at Republic Steel in Chicago killed 10 workers. Roosevelt incurred the wrath of John L. Lewis by failing to support the strikers and Roosevelt pronounced "a plague on both your houses," the C.I.O., and "Little Steel."

June 1

Retirement of Associate Justice Willis Van Devanter gave Roosevelt his first chance to make an appointment to the Supreme Court. Senator Hugo L. Black of Alabama was nominated and confirmed August 12 although charged with once being a member of the Ku Klux Klan. Black had a record of supporting the President's New Deal policies.

A bill to permit renewal of 5 year term insurance for servicemen, vetoed by the President, was put into law by overriding the veto.

July 7

When Japan began full-scale invasion of China at Peking Roosevelt refused to recognize that a state of war existed, because the provisions of the Neutrality Act would prevent him from aiding China.

July 14

Death of Senate Majority Leader Joseph T. Robinson of Arkansas removed Roosevelt's chief supporter in his "court packing" plan.

July 16

Secretary Hull circularized the governments of the world asking them to subscribe to his "Eight Pillars of Peace," enunciated at the Buenos Aires conference. Like the Kellogg-Briand Pact which it included, it was meaningless without action.

July 22

Referral to committee finally killed the "court packing" bill. Roosevelt had suffered a major defeat, although he later claimed to have won the "war."

	Signed the Bankhead-Jones Farm Tenant Act, providing loans for farm tenants and sharecroppers, as well as aid for migrant workers.
August 18	Signed the Miller-Tydings Enabling Act, although unenthusiastic about its "price fixing" provisions.
August 26	Signed the Revenue Act of 1937 which attempted to plug some loopholes in some income taxes.
September 1	Signed the National Housing Act (Wagner-Steagall) creating the United States Housing Authority (USHA) to promote slum clearance and housing projects.
September 11	Bernard Baruch, after return from Europe, visited Roosevelt at Hyde Park and told him that anything could happen.
October 5	In Chicago speech stated that "the epidemic of world lawlessness" suggested that the world community "quarantine the aggressors." Outbursts by isolationists forced Roosevelt to deny that he meant American participation in collective security.
October 12	Called for a special session of Congress to convene November 15 to deal with economic reform. An economic recession had begun in the summer.
October 18	Appointed Nathan Straus to the Housing Authority Administration.
November 15	Submitted message to special session of Congress calling for legislation to deal with agriculture, with standards for wages and hours and with conservation of national resources. Conservatives blocked all measures.
Nov. 29-Dec. 6	Fishing trip to Florida Keys on U.S.S. Potomac.
December	Still hoped to cut spending and balance the budget during the recession. Told cabinet to "sit tight and keep quiet."

December 8   Appointed Joseph Kennedy ambassador to Great Britain
                    to succeed the ailing Robert Bingham. Bingham died
                    on December 18.

December 12   Japanese planes sunk the United States gunboat Panay
                    on the Yangtze River, killing two Americans. Japan
                    formally apologized and paid $2 million in reparations.

                                        1938
January 3   Annual message to Congress promised action against
                    special interests and called for preparedness for self-
                    defense in view of the world situation.

January 4   In press conference seemed to favor a "cartel" ap-
                    proach, indicating differences between his advisors
                    and in his own thinking about monopolies.

January 6   Sent message to Speaker of the House William B. Bank-
                    head opposing the Ludlow Resolution (January 10, 1935)
                    as crippling the President's power to conduct foreign
                    policy. The resolution was killed by referral back to
                    committee.

January 13   Appointed Hugh Wilson ambassador to Germany to suc-
                    ceed William Dodd.

January 15   Nominated Stanley F. Reed of Kentucky to the Supreme
                    Court to fill the vacancy created by the retirement of
                    Justice George Sutherland on January 18. Confirmed
                    by the Senate on January 25.

January 17   National Foundation for the Fight on Infantile Paralysis
                    (March of Dimes) established with F.D.R. founder and
                    Basil O'Connor national chairman. Celebrations planned
                    for the President's birthday, January 30.

February 16   Signed the Agricultural Adjustment Act replacing the
                    earlier one declared unconstitutional. Quotas, includ-
                    ing an "ever-normal granary," were kept, but proces-
                    sing taxes eliminated. A Federal Crop Insurance Cor-
                    poration was established.

March 3   Answered John Maynard Keynes' letter of February 1, with little indication he was aware of Keynes' views on the recession.

March 4   Appointed Adolph A. Berle, Jr., of New York Assistant Secretary of State.

March 5   Appointed Thurman Arnold Assistant United States Attorney General to replace Robert H. Jackson. Arnold vigorously prosecuted anti-trust cases.

March 18   President Lázaro Cárdenas of Mexico announced the nationalization of United States and British oil holdings valued at 450 million dollars. Secretary Hull demanded fair compensation.

April 14   Asked Congress to embark on a spending program, and defended his reversal of policy in a "fireside chat" that night.

April 29   Asked Congress for an investigation of a concentration of economic power.

April 30-May 8   Cruise on U.S.S. Philadelphia to West Indies and Virgin Islands.

May 11   Signed bill giving primary power to lease mineral lands to Indian councils or government.

May 17   Signed the Naval Expansion Act authorizing the construction of a two ocean navy over the next ten years.

May 26   The House Committee on Un-American Activities was established with its chairman Martin Dies of Texas. Roosevelt was generally opposed to its investigations.

May 27   The Revenue Act of 1938 became law without the President's signature. It cut taxes on large corporations.

June 7-10   Received King George VI and Queen Elizabeth of Great
                   Britain in Washington, then entertained them "on hot
                   dogs" at Hyde Park.

June 16   A joint legislative-executive Temporary National Eco-
                   nomic Committee (TNEC) was established to deal with
                   monopolies as requested by the President on April 29.
                   Senator Joseph C. O'Mahoney of Wyoming was its chair-
                   man, with Leon Henderson representing the President.

June 24   Signed the Food, Drug and Cosmetic Act (Wheeler-Lea)
                   requiring manufacturers to list ingredients on labels
                   and prohibiting false or misleading advertising.

                   In "fireside chat" denounced "Copperheads" in his party
                   and began attack on Southern conservatives in barn-
                   storming tour of country. Among those he attacked
                   were Senators Walter George of Georgia, "Cotton Ed"
                   Smith of South Carolina, and Millard Tydings of Mary-
                   land. All won in November.

June 25   Signed a Fair Labor Standards Act establishing a mini-
                   mum wage of 40 cents an hour, time-and-a-half for
                   work over 40 hours per week, and forbidding child labor.

July 14   Reviewed fleet in San Francisco Bay.

July 16-Aug. 9   Cruised on U.S.S. Houston from San Diego to Galapagos
                   Island, returning through Panama Canal to Pensacola,
                   Florida.

August 18   On trip to Canada to dedicate the Thousand Island Bridge
                   stated that "the People of the United States will not stand
                   idly by if domination of Canadian soil is threatened by
                   any other empire.

September 26   Sent cables to Hitler and Mussolini pleading for peace.

September 30   In Munich Conference "peace in our time" was achieved for a very short time when British Prime Minister Neville Chamberlain and French Premier Edouard Daladier granted Hitler the Sudetenland. Roosevelt had little faith in this "appeasement."

October 6   Instructed Joseph C. Grew, American ambassador to Japan, to deliver a strong protest to the Japanese for violating the Open Door policy.

October 16   Appointed Norman Davis as the American delegate to the forthcoming Brussels Conference to discuss Japanese aggression.

November 8   Congressional elections proved rather disastrous for the New Deal and for Roosevelt. Republicans gained 80 seats in the House and 7 in the Senate. Roosevelt's attempted "purge" was a failure.

November 24   The United States joined other nations in a mild, ineffectual rebuke of Japan at the Brussels Conference.

December 24   In the Lima (Peru) Declaration the 21 American nations pledged to support republican governments and to resist foreign intervention.

Harry L. Hopkins appointed to succeed Daniel C. Roper as Secretary of Commerce. Confirmed, after bitter debate, on January 23.

Appointed Colonel Francis C. Harrington Administrator of the Works Progress Administration.

December 31   Ambassador Grew was ordered to deliver a second protest to Japan after the Japanese reply to the October 6 note argued that a "new situation" made the Open Door policy no longer applicable.

1939

January 1   Frank Murphy of Michigan replaced Homer S. Cummings as Attorney General.

January 4   Annual message to Congress was devoted almost entirely to problems in foreign affairs. His following budget proposals called for increased spending for national defense. He called for a repeal of the arms embargo.

January 5   Felix Frankfurter of Massachusetts appointed Associate Justice of the Supreme Court. Confirmed January 17.

January 23   Crash of new American bomber in California took several lives, including a French Air Force officer. Protests by isolationists forced the President to state, on January 27, that he had approved a sale of planes to France. In private, a few days later, referred to the American frontier as "on the Rhine."

February 3   In press conference stated American fundamentals as unchanged, against entangling alliances and for a peaceful world.

February 27   Eleanor Roosevelt announced resignation from the Daughters of the American Revolution over refusal to permit use of hall by Negro singer Marian Anderson.

March 4   Laurence Steinhardt succeeded Joseph Davies as ambassador to the Soviet Union.

March 8   Appointed Harold D. Smith as Director of the Budget.

March 20   William O. Douglas of Minnesota, Chairman of the Securities and Exchange Commission, appointed Associate Justice to the Supreme Court.

April 3   Signed the Administrative Reorganization Act calling for more efficient government by regrouping various agencies. Effected by Executive Order on July 1 and on September 8.

April 9	On leaving Warm Springs flippantly remarked: "I'll be back in autumn if we don't have a war."
April 14	Addressed open letter to Hitler and Mussolini asking them to avow friendly relations with their neighbors. They denied aggressive intentions.
April 15	In a Pan-American Day speech placed the Monroe Doctrine in terms of continental solidarity to warn the Old World's aggressors.
April 27	Told Secretary Hull that Constantine A. Oumansky would be acceptable as the Soviet Ambassador and jokingly added "but double the guard."
April 30	Opened New York World's Fair. First television appearance of a President.
May 19	Told Congressmen that repeal of the arms embargo and reinstatement of "cash and carry" (expired May 1) might save Europe.
June 30	Signed the Emergency Relief Appropriation Act, providing funds for WPA (now changed to Works Projects Administration). The Act abolished the Federal Theater Project without objection from the President. Earlier requests for additional relief funds were scaled down by Congress.
July 1	By Executive Order set up the Federal Security Agency, the Federal Works Agency, and the Federal Loan Agency, regrouping 50 government bodies.
	Appointed General George C. Marshall acting Chief of Staff. The post became permanent on September 1.
July 7	Secretary of the Navy Claude A. Swanson died. Succeeded by Assistant Secretary Charles Edison of New Jersey.

July 14   Sent message to Congress pleading for a repeal of the Neutrality Act.

July 18   Senator Borah told Secretary Hull that there would be no war in Europe and that his (Borah's) sources of information in Europe were better than Hull's. The Senate adjourned without taking action on repeal of the Neutrality Act.

July 26   Announced the required six months' notice of termination of the treaty with Japan. Economic sanctions could then be imposed.

August 2   Signed the Hatch Act forbidding Federal office holders below the policy-making level to participate in political campaigns.

August 10   Signed amendment to the Social Security Act extending coverage and postponing increased taxes.

August 23   Germany and the Soviet Union signed a non-aggression pact.

August 24   Appealed once more to Hitler and Mussolini to keep the peace.

September 1   Germany invaded Poland, beginning World War II. Great Britain and France declared war on Germany on September 3.

September 3   In "fireside chat" told American people that this country would remain neutral but that he could not ask them to remain neutral in thought.

September 5   Proclaimed United States neutrality under the Neutrality Act of 1937.

September 8   Proclaimed a "limited" national emergency.

Executive Order 8248 created the Executive Office of the President, then to be staffed by six administrative assistants but in later years to be expanded to include such important agencies as the National Security Council, the Central Intelligence Agency, and the Council of Economic Advisors.

September 16   Signed the Burke-Wadsworth bill, providing for the first peacetime compulsory military training in the United States.

September 21   Called for a special session of Congress to repeal the arms embargo.

October 2   The Declaration of Panama by 21 American nations proclaimed a safety zone around the Americas.

October 10   Sweden appealed to Roosevelt to use his influence to halt a threatening Russian pressure on Finland. The President cabled Ambassador Steinhardt a message the next day to present to President Kalinin of the Soviet Union.

October 11   Informed by Albert Einstein about the possibility of Germany developing an atomic bomb.

November 4   Signed the Neutrality Act of 1939 authorizing "cash and carry" of arms and munitions to belligerents. Empowered the President to establish combat zones into which American ships could not go.

November 16   Death of Associate Justice Pierce Butler gave Roosevelt a chance to replace another conservative on the Supreme Court.

November 30   Finland invaded by the Soviet Union. Roosevelt, returning to Washington the next day, called it "this dreadful rape," and later a "wanton disregard for law." 98

per cent of Americans agreed, he said, and on December 2 he hoped for a "moral embargo" of airplanes or airplane equipment to nations bombing civilian populations.

December	Aid for Finland supported by Roosevelt, but military supplies not included for fear of incurring wrath of isolationists.
December 1	Mrs. Roosevelt attended hearing of the American Youth Congress at the House Committee on Un-American Activities (the Dies Committee) and took some young members of the Youth Congress to lunch at the White House.
December 23	Addressed Christmas letter to Pope Pius XII, hoping for a peaceful world. Appointed Myron C. Taylor as his personal representative to the Vatican with the rank of Ambassador.
December 28	Appointed Sumner Welles as temporary chairman of a special State Department Committee to study questions of peace and the post war world. It became the Advisory Committee on Problems of Foreign Relations on January 8, with Welles continuing as Chairman. It submitted a memorandum to Roosevelt on January 12, termed Organization of Neutrals.

1940

January 3	In State of the Union message urged an end to isolationism and an interest in organizations to promote future peace. This did not mean, he said, that this country should involve itself in war.
January 4	Frank Murphy, the Attorney General, appointed to the Supreme Court to succeed Pierce Butler. Robert H. Jackson appointed Attorney General.
January 16	Appealed to leaders in Congress to grant credit to the Finns. This modest proposal was opposed by Secretary Hull, and the request for non-military aid met

strong opposition in Congress. Finland fell to the Soviets in March.

January 26   The Trade Treaty of 1911 with Japan was allowed to lapse. Shipments of oil, scrap iron and steel were curtailed or halted.

February 1   Wrote Winston Churchill concerning fears of encroachment upon our neutrality -- the sinking of the German Graf Spee by the British the preceding December being the occasion.

February 8   Wrote Secretary of the Interior Ickes, who had submitted his resignation in anger: "You and I have been married for better or worse for too long to get a divorce or for you to break up a home. I continue to need you." Ickes withdrew his resignation.

February 10   Spoke to delegates to the American Youth Congress on White House lawn and was booed by the pacifistic, isolationist, and often pro-Communist group.

March 8   Mrs. Roosevelt was named the most popular woman in the world by a Gallup poll.

April 10   German attack on Norway caused Roosevelt to extend the provisions of the Neutrality Act to that area. He also "froze" Norwegian and Danish funds in the United States to deny them to the aggressors.

April 13   Publicly denounced German aggression against Denmark and Norway.

May 10   Warned Congress that the dictator states had a wild dream of conquering the whole earth.

May 15   Winston Churchill, who had replaced Chamberlain on May 10, sent Roosevelt a frank assessment of the British situation, asking for destroyers and aircraft. He corresponded regularly with the President during the war, signing his letters "Former Naval Person."

May 16   Sent special message to Congress stating that the American people must recast their thinking about national protection. He called for more than a billion dollars in additional appropriations and for the production of 50,000 combat planes a year. Congress passed the bills within the month.

May 20   Secretary of the Navy Edison resigned. Roosevelt had maneuvered (with Boss Hague of New Jersey) to have him named as candidate for Governor of New Jersey. He wanted the Navy post for either Ambassador to France Bullitt or Colonel Frank Knox, a Republican.

May 25   Established the Office for Emergency Management to coordinate the defense effort.

Received letter from William Allen White, editor of the Emporia Gazette and recent organizer of the Committee to Defend America by Aiding the Allies. White wanted "sailing orders;" to be told what he could do to help.

May 26   In "fireside chat" tried to reassure the American people and to ask them to stand by the democratic process and the gains of the New Deal.

May 28   Set up the National Defense Advisory Commission as an adjunct to the old National Defense Council. The new commission (NDAC) consisted of six prominent New Dealers and business executives and operated without a chairman, although William S. Knudsen, President of General Motors, was put in charge of the vital area of production. Knudsen was frequently at odds with the labor member, Sidney Hillman, President of the Amalgamated Clothing Workers.

May 31   Sent a second message to Congress stating that events of the past two weeks (the German blitzkrieg of the Low Countries) called for more American preparedness. Congress appropriated more money.

May - June   The President was bombarded with pleas for help from leaders in Great Britain and France.

June 3   Using a World War I law, the British were provided with old military equipment, sold by the army to private American concerns and then resold to the British. 600,000 rifles, 800 cannon, and other equipment were made available to replace arms lost in the then-occurring evacuation at Dunkirk, France.

June 10   In a Commencement address at the University of Virginia at Charlottesville Roosevelt delivered a major foreign policy address. He announced that Italy had declared war on almost defeated France: "On this tenth day of June, 1940, the hand that held the dagger has struck it into the back of its neighbor."

June 15   Established a National Defense Research Committee, with Dr. Vannevar Bush as chairman, to coordinate research on new weapons.

June 19   Asked for resignation of Secretary of War Woodring, who had opposed aiding the Allies at the possible cost of weakening our own defenses.

June 20   On the eve of the Republican Convention announced appointments of Republicans Henry L. Stimson of New York as Secretary of War and Frank Knox of Illinois as Secretary of the Navy.

June 24-28   Wendell Willkie of Indiana nominated by the Republicans at Philadelphia on the sixth ballot. Charles L. McNary of Oregon was nominated for Vice President.

June 27   Donald M. Nelson placed in charge of the purchase of war supplies.

Proclaimed the Espionage Act of 1917 to be in effect.

June 28   Signed the Alien Registration Act (Smith Act) requiring more careful scrutiny of aliens. The act also made it unlawful to advocate the overthrow of the government by force or violence, or to organize or belong to any group advocating or teaching such a doctrine.

July 1   In special message to Congress asked for a Selective Service Act to be balanced by a steeply graduated excess profits tax.

July 2   Signed bill which established controls over export of vital materials. Appointed Lieutenant Colonel Russell L. Maxwell as administrator of Exchange Control.

July 15-18 Nominated on first ballot at the Democratic Party Convention at Chicago. Henry A. Wallace of Iowa received the nomination for Vice President.

July 24   Assistant Secretary of War Louis Johnson resigned; replaced by Colonel Stimson's choice, Judge Robert P. Patterson. Roosevelt offered Johnson a post as administrative assistant but he refused.

July 29   Asked Congress for authority to call out the National Guard for extensive training.

July 30   The Act of Havana stated that the 21 American nations would not permit the transfer of any European possession in the New World to any non-American nation.

August 1   Foreign Commissar Vyacheslav of the Soviet Union told the Supreme Soviet: "I will not dwell on our relations with the United States of America, if only for the reason that there is nothing good that can be said about them." Some discussions continued between the two countries, although strained.

August 2   After several weeks of silence came out in support of the Burke-Wadsworth (conscription) bill.

August 7   James A. Farley resigned as Postmaster General ef-
                  fective August 31. He also had resigned earlier as
                  Chairman of the Democratic National Committee, but
                  had agreed to serve until August 17. Edward J. Flynn
                  was selected to fill the latter post.

August 16   Appointed Nelson A. Rockefeller coordinator of com-
                  mercial and cultural relations of the American Repub-
                  lics for Defense Council.

August 18   At Ogdensburg, New York, joined Prime Minister Mac-
                  kenzie King of Canada in statement of collaboration for
                  mutual defense.

August 19   Claude R. Wickard of Indiana appointed Secretary of
                  Agriculture, replacing Henry Wallace.

August 31   Frank C. Walker of Pennsylvania appointed Postmaster
                  General.

September   America First Committee formed, opposed to Roose-
                  velt's increased involvement in aiding the Allies.

September 3   In an Executive Agreement promised to send fifty World
                  War I destroyers in exchange for ninety-nine year
                  leases on bases in Newfoundland, Bermuda and the West
                  Indies. He was much criticized for bypassing the
                  Senate.

September 13   Appointed Jesse H. Jones of Texas to replace Harry
                  Hopkins as Secretary of Commerce. Congress ap-
                  proved bill allowing Jones to continue as Federal Loan
                  Agency head as well.

September 16   Signed the Selective Training and Service Act (Burke-
                  Wadsworth) calling for the registration of all men aged
                  21 to 35. The first peacetime draft in American his-
                  tory set up registration on October 16, with the first
                  draft numbers drawn on October 29.

Sam Rayburn of Texas elected Speaker of the House of Representatives, replacing William B. Bankhead of Alabama who had died the day before.

September 26   Proclaimed an embargo, effective October 16, on all exports of scrap iron and steel to countries outside the Western Hemisphere, except Great Britain.

September 29   Appointed General Lewis B. Hershey as acting draft director.

September 30   Colonel Francis C. Harrington, head of the Works Progress Administration, died.

October 25   John L. Lewis urged labor to vote Republican and threatened to resign as CIO head if Roosevelt were reelected. He resigned after the election.

October 28   Presided over lottery for draft. First number, drawn by Secretary Stimson, 158.

In campaign speech at Madison Square Garden attacked the Republican isolationists in Congressmen, especially that "perfectly beautiful alliteration--Congressmen Martin, Barton and Fish."

October 30   In speech at Boston told American mothers: "I have said this before, but I shall say it again and again and again. Your boys are not going to be sent into any foreign wars."

November 2   In speech at Buffalo stated: "Your President says this country is not going to war."

November 5   Reelected for a precedent-making third term with Henry Wallace as Vice President. They received 27,243,466 votes to Willkie and McNary's 22,304,755. The Socialist Party with Norman Thomas received 99,557 votes and the Communist (Worker's) Party with Earl Browder,

46,251. Roosevelt received 449 electoral votes, carrying 38 states while Willkie received 82 votes, carrying 10 states.

November 22   Appointed Admiral William D. Leahy as ambassador to the Vichy government in Franch. This replacement of William C. Bullitt, who had resigned November 13, was a controversial recognition of the Petain government and a blow to Charles de Gaulle and the Free French.

December 3-14   Inspection cruise through the West Indies on board the U.S.S. Tuscaloosa. First cruise by "Fala," his favorite Scottie. Met Duke of Windsor.

December 8   Churchill wrote to the President, pledging to hold off Hitler while America converted its industries to war production. Payment for the material aid he left to Roosevelt, saying "ways and means will be found." Lend-Lease was the answer found in January.

December 17   In press conference described aid to Great Britain as in the interests of the United States thus "get rid of the silly, foolish old dollar sign." He used the illustration of lending a garden hose to a neighbor whose house was on fire.

December 18   Vetoed the Walter-Logan bill designed to cut the power of independent agencies.

December 29   In "fireside chat" proposed that the United States make itself "the great arsenal of democracy." Warning that a victorious Nazi Germany would pose a threat to the Americas he called for an end to "business as usual" and asked for an all-out effort.

1941

January 6   In Annual Message to Congress proposed the Lend-Lease Bill giving him the power to lend, lease, or otherwise dispose of, to any country whose defense was vital to the United States, up to seven billion dollars worth of arms and supplies. Suggested the Four Freedoms (of speech, of worship, from want, from fear) later incorporated in the Atlantic Charter, August 14, 1941.

January 7   By Executive Order created the Office of Production Management (OPM), to oversee all aspects of defense production. Named dual chairmen, William S. Knudsen and Sidney Hillman.

January 8   Named Admiral Husband E. Kimmel commander in chief of the United States fleet, now to be divided into Atlantic, Pacific, and Asiatic commands.

January 9   Harry L. Hopkins, special envoy of the President, arrived in London to confer with British leaders.

January 16   Requested Congress to appropriate 350 million dollars to build 200 merchant ships.

January 19   Conferred with Wendell Willkie who was about to embark on a visit to Great Britain.

                            THIRD TERM

January 20   Inaugurated, with oath of office administered by Chief Justice Hughes. His speech was a philosophical defense of democracy, which he felt was threatened by events in Europe.

January 22   Associate Justice James C. McReynolds announced his retirement. The President did not fill the vacancy until June.

January 23   Appointed Dean G. Acheson Assistant Secretary of State.

January 24   Welcomed the new British Ambassador, Viscount Halifax, aboard the battleship King George V in Chesapeake Bay.

February 3   The Supreme Court, in U.S. v. Darby Lumber Company, unanimously upheld the Fair Labor Standards Act of June 25, 1938.

February 6   Appointed John Winant ambassador to Great Britain to succeed the "isolationist" Joseph Kennedy.

February 15   Sent James B. Conant, president of Harvard University, on mission to Great Britain to exchange war science information.

February 24   Requested Congress to appropriate almost $4 billion for the army.

February 28   Senator Burton K. Wheeler of Montana attacked the Lend-Lease bill as leading to war and dictatorship in the United States. At various times others opposed Lend-Lease, including Senator Gerald Nye of North Dakota, Joseph P. Kennedy and Charles A. Lindbergh. But speaking for it was Wendell Willkie.

March 8   In "fireside chat" stated that "the democratic way of life" could not survive in the United States if democracy died in the rest of the world.

March 11   Signed the Lend-Lease bill. Urged Congress, the next day, to appropriate $7 billion to aid the democracies. Harry Hopkins was placed in charge of Lend-Lease, without title of administrator.

March 15   Announced the need of a "bridge of ships" across the Atlantic to carry food and arms to those who "are fighting the good fight."

March 19   Created an 11-man board to mediate strikes in defense industries.

Mar. 19-April 1	Inspection tour to the Bahamas on the U.S.S. Potomac.
March 30	Ordered the Coast Guard to seize Italian, German, and Danish ships in American waters.
March 31	The final report of TNEC (established June 16, 1938) recommended new procedures to deal with monopolies.
April 10	Announced an agreement with Danish Minister Henrik de Kaufmann to establish a temporary protectorate over Greenland and to build air bases there.
April 11	Signed bill creating the Office of Price Administration (OPA). Appointed Leon Henderson Administrator.
April 24	Ordered the Navy to protect convoys in the Atlantic Ocean as far as 26° West Longitude.
April 28	Colonel Charles A. Lindbergh resigned commission as a reserve officer in the Air Corps, saying that President Roosevelt's questioning of his loyalty left him no alternative.
May	Created Office of Civilian Defense, with Mayor of New York City Fiorella La Guardia its head.
May 15	Appealed to the French people not to support the Vichy government.
May 21	The Robin Moor, an American merchant ship, was sunk off Brazil by a German submarine. The crew was adrift in lifeboats for four weeks, and the President and American public did not hear the news until mid-June.
May 22	Ordered Admiral Stark to prepare an expedition to seize the Azores from Portugal. He publicly announced, on May 27, the need for such a plan, but it never materialized because Hitler did not move through the Iberian Peninsula to attack Africa.

May 26	Ordered an additional draft of all men who had become 21 after the first registration.
May 27	Proclaimed an "unlimited national emergency."
May 29	Authorized the training of British airmen in the United States.
May 31	Named Secretary of the Interior Ickes as Petroleum Coordinator.
June	The White House was picketed by the Communist group "American Peace Mobilization" to arouse public opposition to the President's policies. The pickets were called off on the night of June 21.
June 2	Chief Justice of the Supreme Court Charles Evans Hughes announced his retirement.
June 7	Returned ABC 1 report, submitted by a joint British-American military team headed by Admiral Stark, without official approval. The report contained plans should the United States be compelled to resort to war.
June 12	Appointed Harlan Fiske Stone, on the Court since 1925, Chief Justice of the Supreme Court, and Senator James F. Byrnes of South Carolina and Attorney General Robert H. Jackson Associate Justices. Named Francis Biddle Attorney General.
June 14	Ordered freezing of all assets in the United States of all Axis and Axis-occupied countries, excluding Japan from the order.
June 22	Germany invaded Russia, and the President promised aid to Russia two days later.
June 25	Executive Order established a Fair Employment Practice Committee which helped to curb discrimination

against Negroes during the war years. A filibuster in the Senate early in 1946 killed an attempt to make it permanent.

June 29   Ordered the induction of 900,000 additional men into the armed forces.

June 30   Dedicated Franklin D. Roosevelt Library at Hyde Park, the depository of his papers.

July 7   Made agreement with Iceland to establish bases there to prevent German occupation.

July 10   Requested that Congress appropriate $4.7 billion additional defense money. The next day asked for $3.3 billion more for the navy and merchant marine.

July 11   Named William J. Donovan head of a new intelligence agency, later to be called the Office of Strategic Services (OSS).

July 17   Froze assets in the United States of Latin American companies having Axis ties.

July 21   Urged Congress to extend the time served by draftees beyond one year.

July 26   After learning that the Japanese had occupied southern Indo-China, the President froze all Japan's assets in the United States.

July 27   Ambassador Grew in Tokyo warned that there were rumors that the Japanese, in case of war, might launch a surprise attack on Pearl Harbor. The Office of Naval Intelligence placed little credence in the rumors.

July 30   Asked Congress for authority to set ceilings on prices to fight inflation.

Harry Hopkins flew to Moscow to confer with Stalin.

Name of Nelson A. Rockefeller's post changed to Office of Coordinator of Inter-American Affairs.

July 31   Named Vice President Wallace to head a newly created Economic Defense Board.

August 1   Ordered a ban on the export of aviation gasoline and oil outside the Western Hemisphere except to Great Britain and other nations resisting aggression.

August 9   Met Prime Minister Churchill at sea off Argentia, New-foundland, Roosevelt traveling on the U.S.S. Augusta and Churchill on the Prince of Wales. Discussed problems and agreed on the "Atlantic Charter," announced August 14. The Charter stated eight points of agreement on war goals, including the "Four Freedoms" (see January 6, 1941).

August 11   Ordered the Federal Reserve Board to restrict installment credit buying.

August 17   Ambassador Kichisaburo Nomura of Japan called on Roosevelt and was warned that further Japanese moves to the south would compel steps toward insuring the safety and security of the United States.

August 18   Signed bill extending the Selective Service for 18 months. The bill had passed the Senate easily, but the House vote was 203-202.

August 28   Appointed Donald M. Nelson, head of Sears Roebuck, to be chairman of a new Supplies Priorities and Allocation Board. Changed the Office of Production Management to an advisory council.

Appointed Edward R. Stettinius, Jr., Lend-Lease Administrator.

August 29   Appointed Ambassador to Great Britain W. Averell
                   Harriman to head the United States delegation to Mos-
                   cow to confer with the British and Russians, beginning
                   September 29.

September 3   Rejected proposal by Prime Minister Fumimaro Konoye
                   of Japan to hold a summit conference on differences.
                   Demanded that Japan agree in advance to give up her
                   New Order in Asia.

September 4   The United States destroyer Greer was attacked by a
                   German submarine while carrying mail to Iceland.
                   Roosevelt, in a press conference the next day, called
                   the attack deliberate.

September 7   Mother, Sara Delano Roosevelt, died at Hyde Park at
                   the age of 86.

September 11   In radio address called German U-boats "the rattle-
                   snakes of the Atlantic" and implied, if not precisely
                   saying, that he was authorizing the Navy to "shoot on
                   sight."

September 16   Appointed David E. Lilienthal chairman of the Tennessee
                   Valley Authority.

September 20   Signed a new tax bill of $3.5 billion.

September 22   Eleanor Roosevelt began work at the New York branch
                   of the Office of Civilian Defense under Mayor La Guar-
                   dia. Often under attack in Congress, she resigned Feb-
                   ruary 20 the next year.

October 3   Stated that he had been prodding the Soviet Union to
                   permit freedom of worship.

October 9   Asked Congress to repeal those sections of the Neu-
                   trality Act that forbade the arming of American mer-
                   chant ships and their entry into belligerent ports.

October 17	A German submarine torpedoed the United States destroyer <u>Kearny</u> off Greenland with a loss of 11 lives.
October 22	Received message from General Robert E. Wood, chairman of the America First committee, asking that questions of war or peace be submitted to a vote of Congress.
October 27	In Navy Day address, carried by radio, the President said, referring to the <u>Kearny</u> torpedoing, "America has been attacked." While saying this would not provoke us to war, he did ask for offensive tactics to guarantee the freedom of the seas.
October 28	Charged by Senator Robert A. Taft of Ohio as having tricked this country onto a road to war.
October 29	Appointed Charles Fahey Solicitor General of the United States.
October 31	The American destroyer <u>Reuben James</u> was torpedoed with a loss of 115 lives.
November 5	Received memorandum from General Marshall and Admiral Stark recommending that the primary objective of Britain and the United States be the defeat of Germany, rather than Japan. The cabinet of the new Japanese Prime Minister, Hideki Tojo, which had replaced the Konoye government on October 16, told the Emperor that Japan would go to war on December 1 if the United States had not resumed trade by then.
November 7	Advised by cabinet that American people would support a war against Japan should she bypass American territory and strike only at British and Dutch possessions. Made no decision whether or not to ask Congressional approval.

November 17   Signed amendment to the Neutrality Act to permit arm-
                   ing of American merchant vessels and allowing Amer-
                   ican ships to enter war zones.

November 19   A Magic (the name for the Japanese code, broken earlier
                   that year) intercept of a message from Tokyo to the
                   embassy in Washington used the phrase "east wind
                   rain" which would be used in a short wave broadcast
                   to indicate "Japan-U.S. relations in danger." The
                   phrase was used on December 4.

                   Announced agreement on difficulties with Mexico, in-
                   cluding a plan to decide the value of expropriated oil
                   holdings.

November 20   Newly arrived Japanese diplomat Saburo Kurusu joined
                   Ambassador Nomura in presenting a new proposal,
                   promising to withdraw troops from Indo-China in ex-
                   change for a resumption of American trade.

November 22   John L. Lewis called off a strike in "captive" coal
                   mines, accepting President Roosevelt's offer to pro-
                   vide arbitration of the union shop issue.

November 25   Appointed William C. Bullitt his special envoy in the
                   Near East.

November 26   Secretary of State Hull replied to the Kurusu-Nomura
                   proposal of November 20 by an ultimatum that Japan
                   get out of China and Indo-China and agree to respect
                   the sovereignty of all nations.

November 27   Commanders of United States forces in the Pacific
                   alerted to the probability of a Japanese attack in the
                   Philippines or in Southeast Asia.

November 28   Plans made by the President and his advisors to appeal
                   to Emperor Hirohito, to send a message to Congress
                   warning it that the United States would have to fight

should Japan attack a third country, and to address such a warning to Japan. Only the first, on December 6, was accomplished before Pearl Harbor.

December 1   The Japanese cabinet rejected the Hull ultimatum; war was decided, and the Pearl Harbor task force, already having sailed, was notified to strike on December 7.

Wrote memorandum to Secretary of State Hull and to Under Secretary Sumner Welles alerting them to the movement of Japanese forces southwards along the coast of Indo-China indicating an attack in that area and probably aimed at the occupation of Thailand.

December 2   Asked Japan for explanation of troop and ship movements in French Indo-China. The reply, received December 5, was that they were only precautionary steps, taken because of Chinese troop movements to the North.

December 6   Appealed to Emperor Hirohito in a dispatch to Tokyo at 9 P.M. "to give thought in this definite emergency to ways of dispelling the dark clouds."

December 7   Japanese attacked Pearl Harbor. The news reached the President shortly after 1:20 P.M., E.S.T.

Nomura and Kurusu delivered Japanese rejection of the November 26 proposals to Hull just after the attack.

December 8   Addressed a joint session of Congress, asking it to declare war on Japan. Called December 7 "a day which will live in infamy." Congress acted with only one dissenting vote.

December 11   Germany and Italy declared war on the United States. Congress unanimously responded on the same day.

December 15   Accused Emperor Hirohito of "personal complicity" in the attack on Pearl Harbor.

December 16   Appointed Byron Price director of United States censorship.

December 17   Named Admiral Chester W. Nimitz commander in chief of the Pacific Fleet, replacing Admiral Kimmel. The commander of the United States Army in Hawaii, General Walter C. Short was replaced by General Delos C. Emmons.

Dec. 22-Jan. 12   Churchill and military advisors met with Roosevelt and staff in Washington. One of the plans discussed was a joint operation in North Africa. Code name for conference was Arcadia. Churchill addressed a joint session of Congress on December 26.

December 27   Rationing was ordered on automobile tires. Other goods were put on the ration list in 1942, with coupon books.

December 28   Promised the Philippines that their freedom would be regained.

December 30   Stated that $50 billion, half of the national income of the United States, would be used for war production.

1942

January 1   United Nations Declaration signed by 26 nations in Washington. The nations affirmed the principles of the Atlantic Charter and pledged to make no separate peace with the enemy.

January 6   State of the Union message dealt with the need to increase production to meet the needs of war. Stated that $56 billion would be spent in the next fiscal year for prosecuting the war.

January 12   Signed bill creating the National War Labor Board (NWLB), a 12 member board under William H. Davis, to try to prevent strikes by mediation and arbitration of disputes.

Roosevelt at about this time began a pattern of escapes from the White House: long pilgrimages to Hyde Park, in the summer to Shangri-La, a camp north of Washington, and apparently, until his death, frequent meetings with Lucy Mercer Rutherford.

January 13   Appointed Donald M. Nelson head of the War Production Board (WPB) with supreme power over the economy. The Office of Production Management was replaced.

January 20   Signed a wartime daylight saving bill, to go into effect on February 9.

January 30   Signed the Emergency Price Control Act giving the Office of Price Administration under Leon Henderson power to fix prices and control rents.

February 7   By Executive Order created the War Shipping Administration with Rear Admiral Emory S. Land as its head.

February 9   Appointed Admiral William H. Standley ambassador to the Soviet Union.

February 10   Vetoed an alien registration act as too repressive and illiberal.

February 19   Authorized the Secretary of War to exclude persons from restricted military areas. 110,000 Japanese or Japanese-Americans on the West Coast were placed in relocation centers.

                Named Brigadier General Dwight D. Eisenhower chief of United States War Plans Division.

February 22   In a Washington's Birthday address over radio gave the American equivalent to Winston Churchill's "blood, sweat, and tears."

March 2   Appointed Lieutenant General Henry H. Arnold com-
               mander of the United States Air Force; Lieutenant Gen-
               eral Lesley J. McNair, commander of ground forces;
               Lieutenant General Brehon B. Somervell commander
               of supply services; under the overall command of Gen-
               eral George C. Marshall, Chief of Staff.

March 9   Named Admiral Ernest J. King to succeed Admiral
               Harold R. Stark as Chief of Naval Operations as well
               as keeping his post as commander in chief of the fleet.

March 10   Named Lieutenant General Joseph W. Stilwell chief of
               United Nations operations in China.

March 14   Asked for cut in speed limit to 40 miles per hour to
               conserve rubber.

March 17   Ordered General MacArthur to leave Philippines and
               go to Australia, but to resume the offensive as soon as
               possible. Major General Jonathan M. Wainwright was
               named commander in the Philippines.

March 27   Signed War Powers Bill, providing criminal penalties
               for violation of government priority orders and giving
               the President power to seize certain properties.

March 28   Suspended anti-trust suits against industries engaged
               in war production until end of war.

April 1   Met for first time with the Pacific War Council, com-
               posed of representatives of Allies in that area.

April 3   Named Carlton J. H. Hayes, history professor at Co-
               lumbia, to be ambassador to Spain.

April 14   Appointed Vice President Henry Wallace head of the
               Board of Economic Warfare, in charge of stockpiles of
               essential materials.

April 17   Recalled Ambassador Leahy from Vichy, France, to indicate disapproval of the Laval government.

April 18   By Executive Order established a War Manpower Commission to effectively utilize available manpower. Appointed Federal Security Administrator Paul V. McNutt, former governor of Indiana, chairman of the 9 man board.

April 27   Asked Congress for anti-inflation measures including a $25 thousand limit on individual incomes.

May 15   Signed bill creating the Women's Auxiliary Army Corps (WAACS). Mrs. Oveta Culp Hobby named commander.

May 16   Ordered the release of Earl Browder, Communist party leader, from prison.

May 19   Awarded the Congressional Medal of Honor to Brigadier General James H. Doolittle for leading the air strike against Tokyo on April 18.

May 20   Ex-President Hoover asked that President Roosevelt be given dictatorial powers to win the war.

May 29   Foreign Commissar Molotov signed a Lend-Lease Agreement promising to return material remaining at the end of the war. The President talked to Molotov about a "second front," deemed essential by the Russians, and seemed to promise a cross-channel attack later that year.

June   Entertained several groups of royal exiles either at White House or at Hyde Park, including King Peter of Yugoslavia, King George of Greece, and Queen Wilhelmina of the Netherlands.

June 2   Asked Congress to declare war against Rumania, Bulgaria and Hungary. Congress unanimously did so the next day.

June 13   Grouped several government agencies into an Office of
                         War Information (OWI) and named news commentator
                         Elmer Davis as its head.

                         Signed bill creating the Office of Strategic Services,
                         with intelligence chief William J. Donovan continuing
                         as its head.

June 18-27   Met with Churchill at Hyde Park and then with Soviet
                         and Chinese representatives in Washington to discuss
                         strategy. During the summer was besieged by appeals
                         from Gandhi and Nehru to support Indian independence.
                         Roosevelt had sent Louis Johnson to India as his per-
                         sonal emissary.

June 24   Appointed General Dwight D. Eisenhower commander
                         of United States forces in Europe.

June 27   J. Edgar Hoover, FBI head, announced capture of 8
                         Nazi saboteurs landed on Long Island and Florida from
                         submarines. The President appointed a secret military
                         tribunal to try the spies, 6 of whom were executed and
                         2 given long prison terms.

July 16   The NWLB granted workers a 15 per cent wage increase
                         to match the rise in the cost of living since January,
                         1941. This was known as the "Little Steel Formula,"
                         and costs rose.

July 21   Named Admiral William D. Leahy, whom he had re-
                         called from Vichy, France in April, as his personal
                         Chief of Staff.

July 29   Urged a national service war measure to mobilize all
                         available men and women.

July 30   Signed bill creating the women's auxiliary for the Navy
                         (WAVES). Dr. Mildred Helen McAfee, president of
                         Wellesley College, named its commander.

August 6   Vetoed a synthetic rubber bill. Appointed a fact-finding committee under Bernard M. Baruch to investigate the growing rubber shortage.

August 12-15   W. Averell Harriman represented the President at the First Moscow Conference, with Churchill and Stalin both attending. Stalin was informed that a second front was impossible in 1942.

August 13   Appointed Brigadier General Leslie R. Groves to command the Manhattan Project to develop an atomic bomb.

August 21   In a news conference reported on German atrocities, and said that when the war was over they would have to stand in court and answer for their acts. This laid the groundwork for the Nuremberg Trials.

September 7   Told Congress that if it did not put a ceiling on wages and prices he would do it himself.

September 15   Appointed William M. Jeffers to be in charge of the United States rubber program.

Sept. 17-Oct. 1   Inspection tour by train to the West Coast. Returned through the South.

October 2   Signed bill to "so far as practicable" stabilize wages, salaries, and prices as of the level of September 15.

October 3   Appointed Supreme Court Justice James F. Byrnes head of the Office of Economic Stabilization with power over all economic aspects of the war effort. Byrnes resigned from the Court.

October 7   In memorandum to Mrs. Roosevelt asked that costs of food and servants in the White House be cut in view of higher prices and taxes.

Oct.-Nov.   Eleanor Roosevelt flew to England to make her first wartime good will visit.

November 3   Midterm elections gave Republicans large gains in Congress, the President having played a hands-off role.

Nov. 8-Dec. 1   Operation Torch, the Allied invasion of North Africa, was commanded by General Eisenhower. Roosevelt was much criticized for dealing with Admiral Jean-François Darlan, representing Vichy France and regarded as a leading collaborationist. Eisenhower and Roosevelt did not like to deal with Darlan, but thought it would save American lives. Darlan's assassination on December 24 ended the uproar.

November 13   Signed amendment to the draft bill lowering the draft age from 20 to 18.

November 17   Stated that the French alone would determine the form of their post-war government, but defended General Eisenhower's use of Admiral Darlan in North Africa.

December 4   Ordered the end of the Works Progress Administration, giving it, as he put it, an "honorable discharge."

December 5   Gave Manpower Director Paul V. McNutt broad powers over the draft in an attempt to solve the manpower problem.

1943

January 7   In State of the Union message asked Congress to consider the needs of a post-war world to provide for "freedom from want."

January 11   In budget message asked for $109 billion for the next year.

Wiley B. Rutledge of Iowa appointed to the Supreme Court to succeed James F. Byrnes.

Signed treaty with China abandoning the right of extraterritoriality.

Named former senator from Michigan Prentiss M. Brown as OPA administrator to replace Leon Henderson who had resigned.

Flew from Miami to Africa to attend the Casablanca Conference.

January 14-24   Participated in Casablanca Conference, arriving at a compromise on location of a second front - Sicily and Italy, with the British view of a "soft underbelly" attack in the Balkans, and the United States view of an invasion of France left for a later decision. Attending the conference, in addition to Roosevelt and Churchill were, among others, General Charles de Gaulle, General George C. Marshall, and General Dwight D. Eisenhower. The latter was given command of the North African Theater of operations.

January 28   Met President Getulio Vargas of Brazil on destroyer off Natal, Brazil, to set common defense aims.

February 9   Declared a minimum work week of 48 hours in areas of labor shortage, with time-and-a-half over 40 hours.

February 17-28   Madame Chiang Kai-shek stayed at White House after hospital treatment in New York and a stay at the Roosevelt home in Hyde Park. In speeches to Congress she asked for more decisive strikes against Japan. The President promised China more arms "as fast as the Lord will let us."

March 10   Asked Congress to act on National Resources Planning Board reports recommending "cradle to grave" social security and more government participation in business.

March 11   Signed bill extending Lend-Lease for another year.

March 25   Named Chester C. Davis as Food Administrator.

April 8	Issued an Executive Order to "hold the line" on prices and wages in an attempt to stem inflation. The Consumers' Price Index had risen 25 per cent from August, 1939. It was to rise only 10 per cent from this time to July, 1946.
April 13-29	Inspection tour by train to the Southwest. Met Mexican President Avila Camacho at Monterrey on April 20.
May 1	Ordered Secretary of the Interior Ickes to take over eastern coal mines. John L. Lewis, head of the United Mine Workers, had defied the no-strike pledge and called a strike of 500,000 workers for that day. Lewis called off the strike on May 2 and submitted his case to the WLB.
May 12-25	"Trident" Conference at Washington, attended by Prime Minister Churchill, set date for Normandy invasion as May 1, 1944.
May 18	Addressed the United Nations food conference at Hot Springs, Virginia.
May 27	Issued Executive Order requiring that non-discrimination clauses be incorporated in all Federal war contracts.
May 28	Appointed James F. Byrnes head of a new Office of War Mobilization with power over all areas of the war effort on the home front.
June 3	Ordered striking mine workers to return to work within four days. John L. Lewis called off the strike on June 7.
June 9	Signed the Current Tax Payment act, providing withholding of 20 per cent of taxable income by employers, effective July 1.

June 11	John L. Lewis again called a strike of mine workers when the WLB refused to break the Little Steel Formula to benefit the miners. Roosevelt threatened to draft the miners and once more Lewis called off a strike.
June 20	Ordered use of Federal troops to quell race riots in Detroit.
June 25	The President's veto of a War Labor Disputes Act (Smith-Connally) to prevent strikes in defense industries, was overridden by Congress.
June 28	Chester C. Davis resigned as Food Administrator over anti-inflation policies. He was replaced by Marvin Jones.
June 29	A name-calling fight erupted within the President's official family between Vice President Wallace and Secretary of Commerce Jones.
July 7	Rudolph Forster, Executive Clerk and Administrative Officer in Charge of Executive Papers at the White House, died. He had been at the White House since McKinley's time, March 5, 1897. General Henri Giraud arrived in Washington to meet with President Roosevelt.
July 15	Abolished the Board of Economic Warfare, creating a new office of Economic Warfare under the direction of Leo T. Crowley, chairman of the Federal Deposit Insurance Corporation. The President was attempting to stop the bickering between his officials, particularly Vice President Wallace and Secretary of Commerce Jones.
July 28	Hailed fall of Mussolini as the "first crack in the Axis."
Aug.-Sept.	Eleanor Roosevelt made extensive good-will tour of the Pacific war zone.

August 10   Roosevelt was advised by William C. Bullitt, former
                   ambassador to Russia and now a foreign policy advisor,
                   to stop trying to appease the Russians and to shift mil-
                   itary strategy to the Balkans to bar the Red Army from
                   overrunning much of Europe.

August 12-14   Winston Churchill visited Hyde Park prior to "Quadrant"
                   Conference in Canada.

August 16-26   Attended "Quadrant" Conference at Quebec, Canada
                   discussing future military strategy with the British.

September 7   In message to Congress and in broadcast to the Amer-
                   ican people called for taxes to limit incomes to $25,000
                   a year.

September 25   By Executive Order created the Foreign Economic Ad-
                   ministration, merging several agencies including Lend-
                   Lease. Leo T. Crowley, director of the absorbed Of-
                   fice of Economic Warfare, became administrator.

                   Appointed Edward R. Stettinius, Jr., Under Secretary
                   of State to replace Sumner Welles who had resigned,
                   effective September 30. Welles had been the subject
                   of rumor mongers, and William C. Bullitt, foreign
                   policy advisor, was blamed for this by President Roose-
                   velt. Bullitt's influence diminished from then on.

October 1   Appointed William Averell Harriman ambassador to
                   the Soviet Union to replace Admiral William H. Standley
                   who had resigned.

October 11   Asked Congress to repeal Chinese immigration exclu-
                   sion laws.

October 19-30   Cordell Hull attended a conference with British and
                   Soviet foreign ministers at Moscow.

October 21   Prentiss M. Brown resigned as administrator of the
                    Office of Price Administration because of ill health.
                    The President named Chester Bowles of Connecticut
                    as his successor.

November 6   Expressed gratification at the actions of the House of
                    Representatives on September 21 (Fulbright Resolution)
                    and the Senate on November 5 (Connally Resolution)
                    favoring participation in an international organization
                    to prevent aggression and preserve peace.

November 9   Presided at ceremony in the White House to dramatize
                    the acceptance by 44 nations of the United Nations Re-
                    lief and Rehabilitation Administration (UNRRA). For-
                    mer Governor of New York Herbert H. Lehman was
                    elected its first director general.

November 11   Left on the U.S.S. Iowa for Algeria, there to fly to
                    Teheran, Iran for conference.

November 14   Accidental torpedo firing from accompanying destroyer
                    just missed the Iowa.

November 22   Talked with Generalissimo and Madame Chiang Kai-
                    shek at Cairo, Egypt. With Churchill, a Declaration
                    of Cairo was drawn up (issued December 1), affirming
                    the intention to fight against Japan until an unconditional
                    surrender. Code name for conference was Sextant.

November 27   Arrived at Teheran. Premier Stalin insisted that the
                    President stay at the Russian Embassy to avoid driving
                    around city for meetings.

Nov. 28-Dec. 1   First conference attended by all three leaders. Stalin
                    stated once more intention to enter the war against
                    Japan and plans were initiated for an international or-
                    ganization to keep the peace. A "Declaration of the
                    Three Powers" was issued on December 1.

December 4-6   With Churchill, met President Ismet Inönü of Turkey
                 in Cairo. Anglo-American-Turkish friendship was
                 firmed.

December 8   At Sicily met Lieutenant Generals George S. Patton and
                 Mark W. Clark.

December 10   Signed bill placing pre-Pearl Harbor fathers at bottom
                 of the draft.

December 13   Marvin H. McIntyre, presidential secretary, died.

December 23   Threatened by a strike of the railway brotherhoods,
                 Roosevelt ordered Stimson to seize the railroads. The
                 Army directed operations for three weeks until arbi-
                 tration was finally successful.

December 24   Announced that General Eisenhower had been named to
                 command the Allied armies in the invasion of Europe.

                 Reported to the nation on his trip. Said he "got along
                 fine" with Stalin.

December 28   At a press conference announced that "Dr. New Deal"
                 had given way to "Dr. Win-the-War."

                                      1944
January 11   In State of the Union message proposed an Economic
                 Bill of Rights for the post-war period, seemingly pro-
                 posing a renewed New Deal, with emphasis on housing,
                 health and education. He also proposed a national ser-
                 vice law for both men and women in addition to selec-
                 tive service for the armed forces. Congress failed to
                 act.

January 24   In a memorandum to Secretary Hull stated his opposition
                 to Indo-China returning to French control. "France
                 has milked it for one hundred years. The people of
                 Indo-China are entitled to something better than that."

February 5   In a press conference with members of the Negro News-
                    paper Publishers Association called for publicity to un-
                    cover discrimination in this country.

February 19   Appointed William D. Hassett a presidential secretary
                    to fill the vacancy left by the death of Marvin H. McIn-
                    tyre. A newspaperman, Hassett had been an important
                    aide since 1935.

February 20   Daughter, Mrs. Anna Boettiger, arrived at White House
                    and was to play a major role in helping the President
                    with his contacts and routine. All four sons were in
                    uniform.

February 22   Wrote a scathing veto message to Congress which had
                    passed a tax bill of only $2.2 billion. Roosevelt had
                    originally asked for $16 billion. He called the bill "re-
                    lief not for needy but for greedy."

February 23   Sent public telegram to the Democratic Majority Leader
                    Alben W. Barkley of Kentucky who had resigned because
                    of the President's veto of the tax bill. Asked the Senate
                    to reelect him to the post and it did.

February 25   The Revenue Act of 1944, vetoed by the President, be-
                    came law when Congress overrode his veto. This was
                    the last of 9 vetoes overridden by Congress since 1933.

March   Given a heart examination at Bethesda, Maryland by
                    Dr. Howard G. Bruenn, Navy cardiologist, whose diag-
                    nosis was that a hypertensive heart disease required
                    treatment, including lessened activity and a low-fat
                    diet. Dr. Bruenn was soon placed on the White House
                    staff and accompanied the President on his major trips,
                    including Yalta.

March 4-28   At the President's insistence, Mrs. Roosevelt made a
                    tour by air of the Caribbean area.

March 9   Indicated that he approved the establishment of a Jewish
                 state in Palestine.

March 31   A "states rights G.I." voting bill became law without
                 the President's signature because he wanted the ballot
                 to be limited to federal offices.

May 6-8   Asked Congress to appropriate $3.5 billion in foreign
                 aid, including Lend-Lease.

June 6   Press Conference (No. 954) dealt almost entirely with
                 the invasion of Europe (Overlord), begun this day.

June 22   Signed the Servicemen's Readjustment Act ("G.I. Bill
                 of Rights"), with its important provisions for loans to
                 acquire homes, farms, and businesses as well as aid
                 to acquire education.

June 26-28   At Chicago the Republicans nominated Thomas E. Dewey
                 of New York for President on the first ballot. John W.
                 Bricker of Ohio was nominated for Vice President.

July 1   Opened, at Bretton Woods, New Hampshire, the United
                 Nations Monetary and Financial Conference, expres-
                 sing hope that it would facilitate economic cooperation
                 and peaceful progress.

July 6-11   General de Gaulle visited Washington, and Roosevelt
                 finally admitted that de Gaulle (and his Committee of
                 National Liberation) was the dominant political authority
                 in France, at least until free elections.

July 11   Announced that he would run for a fourth term if nomi-
                 nated by the Democratic National Convention.

July 14-Aug. 17 Inspection tour to Hawaii and the Aleutians, sailing
                 from San Diego on the U.S.S. Baltimore. Met General
                 MacArthur and Admiral Nimitz at Pearl Harbor on July
                 26. Story circulated, which Roosevelt good-humoredly

denied, that Fala had been left behind on an Aleutian island and that the President had sent a destroyer back after him.

July 19-21   Nominated for a fourth term on the first ballot, receiving 1,086 votes to Harry F. Byrd's 89. James Farley received 1 vote. Harry S Truman of Missouri was nominated as Vice President.

July 31   Marguerite (Missy) A. LeHand, long-time Roosevelt secretary, died.

Aug. 21-Oct. 7 At Dumbarton Oaks, near Washington, plans for a post-war international organization were drawn up.

August 28   Secretary of the Navy Frank Knox died. Succeeded by Under Secretary James V. Forrestal of New York.

September 8   Told press conference he advocated the elimination of cartels, both within and without Germany.

September 9-21 Traveled to Quebec for "Octagon" conference with Prime Minister Churchill. The conference, September 11-16, discussed war strategy and occupation plans for Germany. The Morgenthau plan, which contemplated reducing Germany to an agricultural state, was discussed but later discarded by Roosevelt.

September 19   At a Hyde Park meeting Churchill and Roosevelt decided that the atom bomb development should not be shared with Russia, and that it might, "after mature consideration," be used against the Japanese.

September 23   In campaign speech to the Teamsters Union in Washington effectively used humor (including references to Fala) to ridicule his opponents.

September 29   Accused Argentina of failure to fulfill its inter-American obligations by permitting the spread of Nazi influence in that country.

September 30   Appointed Julius A. Krug as head of the War Production Board to succeed retiring Donald M. Nelson.

October 9-18   The President, not in attendance, was kept informed about discussions at a second Moscow Conference between Stalin and Churchill. Averell Harriman, the United States Ambassador and General John R. Deane, Chief of the United States Military Mission reported on all deliberations. Roosevelt seemed to accept the splitting up of the Balkans into Russian and British spheres of influence, but not the Curzon line as the boundary of Poland.

October 30   Announced recall of General Joseph W. Stilwell from China at the request of Chiang Kai-shek. Replaced by Lieutenant General Albert C. Wedemeyer (with Major General Patrick J. Hurley as Ambassador) in November.

November 2   Appointed Donald M. Nelson his "personal representative" to China to speed the production of war goods.

November 7   Reelected for a fourth term with Harry S Truman Vice President. They received 25,602,504 votes to 22,006,285 received by Dewey and Bricker. Votes for other parties' candidates were negligible. The electoral vote was 432 to 99, with Roosevelt carrying 36 states.

November 30   Secretary of State Cordell Hull resigned because of ill health. Under Secretary Edward R. Stettinius of Virginia succeeded him.

November   Dismissed Assistant Attorney General Norman M. Littell for insubordination, backing his Attorney General, Francis Biddle, with whom Littell had been feuding.

December 16   Signed bill freezing the Social Security Tax at 1 per cent for 1945.

December 18   In Korematsu v. United States the Supreme Court, by
                 a vote of 6-3, upheld the Japanese relocation program
                 as justified by the military emergency. It held unan-
                 imously, however, that Japanese-Americans of unques-
                 tioned loyalty could not be retained.

December 27   Took over railroads to prevent strike. Returned to
                 private management on January 18, 1945.

                 Ordered the Army to take over the Montgomery Ward
                 headquarters in Chicago for refusing to obey the Na-
                 tional War Labor Board. Earlier, Sewell Avery, the
                 president of the company and a vigorous anti-New Deal-
                 er, had been carried out of his office by soldiers.

                                   1945
January 3   Russian Foreign Secretary Molotov formally handed
                 Ambassador Harriman a request for a $6 billion post-
                 war loan, actually to be in credit for manufactured
                 goods. Harriman advised against the loan, without gain-
                 ing political concessions, while Morgenthau favored it.
                 The request was finally declared "lost," and eventually
                 it became a casualty of the Cold War.

January 6   In State of the Union message forecast victory in the
                 war and called for a world organization to promote
                 peace.

January 12   Asked Congress to provide for post-war employment
                 by building a 34,000 mile superhighway system.

                             FOURTH TERM

January 3   War Production Board Chairman J. A. Krug reported
                 that 96,369 airplanes had been turned out in the United
                 States in 1944. Roosevelt's "pipe dream" had been
                 ridiculed for asking for 50,000 a year.

January 6   Annual message to Congress declared that victory over
                   the Axis powers was in sight, but asked for a national
                   service law to fully mobilize the nation's manpower as
                   the war enters a critical phase.

                   Submitted his fourth wartime budget, calling for an ap-
                   propriation of 83 billion dollars for 1945-46 (compared
                   with almost 100 billion dollars the preceding year).
                   His 13 budgets totalled 461 billion dollars, almost four
                   times the combined budgets of all his 30 predecessors
                   in office.

January 19   Received resignation of John Collier, Commissioner of
                   Indian Affairs since 1933. Appointed William A. Brophy
                   as his successor.

January 20   Inaugurated by Chief Justice Stone. His speech of six
                   minutes was one of the shortest inaugural addresses
                   in history, only Washington's second being shorter.
                   He said that we had learned that we can no longer live
                   alone, but must be citizens of the world.

January 22   Nominated Henry A. Wallace as Secretary of Commerce,
                   to replace Jesse Jones whose resignation he had re-
                   quested on Inauguration Day. Jones represented the
                   conservative faction of the Democratic Party.

January 23   Left Newport News, Virginia on the U.S.S. Quincy, to
                   sail to Malta en route to the Yalta Conference.

February 3   Arrived at Yalta, in the Crimea, by air from Malta.

February 4-11   Attended the Yalta Conference with Prime Minister
                   Churchill and Premier Stalin, and key advisors, in-
                   cluding Secretary of State Stettinius, Foreign Ministers
                   Eden and Molotov. A communique was issued on the
                   last day, but most of the decisions were kept secret
                   until after the war.

February 12   Urged Congress to take prompt action on the Bretton Woods proposals, declaring that United States participation in a world fund and bank were essential for a peaceful and prosperous world.

February 13   Named the delegation to represent the United States at the San Francisco Conference to organize the United Nations: Secretary of State Stettinius, Cordell Hull, Senators Connally and Vandenberg, Representatives Sol Bloom of New York and Charles A. Eaton of New Jersey, and Dean Virgina Gildersleeve of Barnard College.

Received King Farouk of Egypt and Emperor Haile Selassie of Ethiopia aboard the U.S.S. Quincy in Great Bitter Lake, Egypt, to which he had flown from Yalta.

February 14   Received King Ibn Saud of Saudi Arabia aboard the Quincy. Ibn Saud told the President that Arabs would choose to die rather than yield their land to the Jews. Roosevelt promised he would do nothing to assist the Jews against the Arabs. Privately he expressed dismay at the Arabs' hard position.

De Gaulle refused to go to Algiers to meet Roosevelt, saying it was "too far away from Paris."

February 20   Major General Edwin M. Watson, the President's military aide for twelve years, died at sea of a cerebral hemorrhage. The Quincy left Algiers on February 18 and arrived at Newport News on February 27.

March 1   Addressed Congress on the Yalta Conference. Asked to sit since it would not require him "to carry about ten pounds of steel," an indication of his weariness. Secret provisions were not revealed and were to be highly criticized when disclosed after his death.

After bitter debate the Senate confirmed Henry A. Wallace as Secretary of Commerce by a vote of 56 to 32.

March 2   Approved the Act of Chapultepec, adopted by the American republics (except Argentina) in Mexico City. It stated that an act of aggression against one was aggression against all and specified armed force to deter or repel it.

March 7   Appointed William H. Davis, chairman of the War Labor Board, director of Economic Stabilization.

March 8   Accepted the credentials of Ambassador Alberto Tarchiani of Italy, thus reestablishing diplomatic relations with that country.

March 13   Received message from Churchill indicating great concern over the Soviet position on Poland, calling it "a great failure and utter breakdown of what was settled at Yalta."

March 16   Told Americans to "tighten belts" since it would be necessary to ship foods to war-ravaged countries as a "matter of decency."

March 20   Disclosed that he had ordered the Office of War Mobilization to study the question of a guaranteed annual wage.

March 23   The Senate rejected the President's nomination of Aubrey Williams as Administrator of the Rural Electrification Administration, 52 to 36.

March 24   Sent message to Stalin resenting Soviet charges that deals with the Germans were being made behind Soviet backs. An exchange of messages took place up to Roosevelt's death, all indicating a growing distrust on both sides.

                     Asked Stalin to try to find a way to let Molotov come to the San Francisco Conference (on the United Nations). Stalin did send Molotov as a tribute to Roosevelt after his death.

March 26   Requested authority from Congress to cut tariffs 50 per cent in reciprocal trade agreements.

April 1   Protested to Stalin about the Soviet position on Poland. Stalin's reply on April 7 stated that "Matters on the Polish questions have really reached a dead end."

April 2   Received resignation of James F. Byrnes as director of the Office of War Mobilization and Reconversion. Appointed Fred M. Vinson as his successor.

April 12   Cabled Churchill that they must be firm with Stalin.

                  Suffered a cerebral hemorrhage at Warm Springs, Georgia at 1 P.M. and died at 3:55 P.M., Georgia time.

April 15   Buried in the Rose Garden at Hyde Park.

COMMONWEALTH CLUB SPEECH
September 23, 1932

This campaign speech, delivered by Franklin D. Roosevelt to the Commonwealth Club in San Francisco, is often cited as indicating his social and economic philosophy. Actually, the speech was mostly the work of two members of his Brain Trust, Adolph Berle, Jr. and Rexford Tugwell, and Roosevelt hardly saw it before delivery, and could not have thought deeply about its philosophy. Furthermore, its pessimistic tone was alien to his nature. Yet he must have accepted its premises, and it is particularly important to note the references to the overbuilt industrial system, to the closed frontier with no safety valve, and to the call for restrictions on great industrial and financial combinations.

I count it a privilege to be invited to address the Commonwealth Club. It has stood in the life of this city and state, and it is perhaps accurate to add, the nation, as a group of citizen leaders interested in fundamental problems of government, and chiefly concerned with achievement of progress in government through non-partisan means. The privilege of addressing you, therefore, in the heat of a political campaign, is great. I want to respond to your courtesy in terms consistent with your policy.

I want to speak not of politics but of government. I want to speak not of parties, but of universal principles. They are not political, except in that larger sense in which a great American once expressed a definition of politics, that nothing in all of human life is foreign to the science of politics. . . .

The issue of government has always been whether individual men and women will have to serve some system of government of economics, or whether a system of government and economics exists to serve individual men and women. This question has persistently dominated the discussion of government for many generations. On questions relating to these things men have differed, and for time immemorial it is probable that honest men will continue to differ.

99

The final word belongs to no man; yet we can still believe in change and in progress. Democracy, as a dear old friend of mine in Indiana, Meredith Nicholson, has called it, is a quest, a never-ending seeking for better things, and in the seeking for these things and the striving for them, there are many roads to follow. But, if we map the course of these roads, we find that there are only two general directions.

When we look about us, we are likely to forget how hard people have worked to win the privilege of government. The growth of the national governments of Europe was a struggle for the development of a centralized force in the nation, strong enough to impose peace upon ruling barons. In many instances the victory of the central government, the creation of a strong central government, was a haven of refuge to the individual. The people preferred the master far away to the exploitation and cruelty of the smaller master near at hand.

But the creators of national government were perforce ruthless men. They were often cruel in their methods, but they did strive steadily toward something that society needed and very much wanted, a strong central state, able to keep the peace, to stamp out civil war, to put the unruly nobleman in his place, and to permit the bulk of individuals to live safely. The man of ruthless force had his place in developing a pioneer country, just as he did in fixing the power of the central government in the development of nations. Society paid him well for his services and its development. When the development among the nations of Europe, however, had been completed, ambition, and ruthlessness, having served its term, tended to overstep its mark.

There came a growing feeling that government was conducted for the benefit of a few who thrived unduly at the expense of all. The people sought a balancing – a limiting force. There came gradually, through town councils, trade guilds, national parliaments, by constitution and by popular participation and control, limitations on arbitrary power.

Another factor that tended to limit the power of those who ruled, was the rise of the ethical conception that a ruler bore a responsibility for the welfare of his subjects.

The American colonies were born in this struggle. The American Revolution was a turning point in it. After the revolution the struggle continued and shaped itself in the public life of the country. There were those who because they had seen the confusion which attended the years of war for American independence surrendered to the belief that popular government was essentially dangerous and essentially unworkable. They were honest people, my friends, and we cannot deny that their experience had warranted some measure of fear. The most brilliant, honest and able exponent of this point of view was Hamilton. He was too impatient of slowmoving methods. Fundamentally he believed that the safety of the republic lay in the autocratic strength of its government, that the destiny of individuals was to serve that government, and that fundamentally a great and strong group of central institutions, guided by a small group of able and public spirited citizens could best direct all government.

But Mr. Jefferson, in the summer of 1776, after drafting the Declaration of Independence turned his mind to the same problem and took a different view. He did not deceive himself with outward forms. Government to him was a means to an end, not an end in itself; it might be either a refuge and a help or a threat and a danger, depending on the circumstances. We find him carefully analyzing the society for which he was to organize a government. "We have no paupers. The great mass of our population is of laborers, our rich who cannot live without labor, either manual or professional, being few and of moderate wealth. Most of the laboring class possess property, cultivate their own lands, have families and from the demand for their labor, are enabled to exact from the rich and the competent such prices as enable them to feed abundantly, clothe above mere decency, to labor moderately and raise their families."

These people, he considered, had two sets of rights, those of "personal competency" and those involved in acquiring and possessing property. By "personal competency" he meant the right of free thinking, freedom of forming and expressing opinions, and freedom of personal living each man according to his own lights. To insure the first set of rights, a government must so order its functions as not to interfere with the individual. But even Jefferson realized that the exercise of the property rights might so interfere with the rights of the individual that the government, without whose assistance the property rights could not exist, must intervene, not to destroy individualism but to protect it.

You are familiar with the great political duel which followed, and how Hamilton, and his friends, building towards a dominant centralized power were at length defeated in the great election of 1800, by Mr. Jefferson's party. Out of that duel came the two parties, Republican and Democratic, as we know them today.

So began, in American political life, the new day, the day of the individual against the system, the day in which individualism was made the great watchword of American life. The happiest of economic conditions made that day long and splendid. On the Western frontier, land was substantially free. No one, who did not shirk the task of earning a living, was entirely without opportunity to do so. Depressions could, and did, come and go; but they could not alter the fundamental fact that most of the people lived partly by selling their labor and partly by extracting their livelihood from the soil, so that starvation and dislocation were practically impossible. At the very worst there was always the possibility of climbing into a covered wagon and moving west where the untilled prairies afforded a haven for men to whom the East did not provide a place. So great were our natural resources that we could offer this relief not only to our own people, but to the distressed of all the world; we could invite immigration from Europe, and welcome it with open arms. Traditionally, when a depression came, a new section of land was opened in the West; and even our temporary misfortune served our manifest destiny.

It was in the middle of the 19th century that a new force was released and a new dream created. The force was what is called the industrial revolution, the advance of steam and machinery and the rise of the forerunners of the modern industrial plant. The dream was the dream of an economic machine, able to raise the standard of living for everyone; to bring luxury within the reach of the humblest; to annihilate distance by steam power and later by electricity, and to release everyone from the drudgery of the heaviest manual toil. It was to be expected that this would necessarily affect government. Heretofore, government had merely been called upon to produce conditions within which people could live happily, labor peacefully, and rest secure. Now it was called upon to aid in the consummation of this new dream. There was, however, a shadow over the dream. To be made real, it required use of the talents of men of tremendous will, and tremendous ambition, since by no other force could the problems of financing and engineering and new developments be brought to a consummation.

So manifest were the advantages of the machine age, however, that the United States fearlessly, cheerfully, and, I think, rightly, accepted the bitter with the sweet. It was thought that no price was too high to pay for the advantages which we could draw from a finished industrial system. The history of the last half century is accordingly in large measure a history of a group of financial Titans, whose methods were not scrutinized with too much care, and who were honored in proportion as they produced the results, irrespective of the means they used. The financiers who pushed the railroads to the Pacific were always ruthless, often wasteful, and frequently corrupt; but they did build railroads, and we have them today. It has been estimated that the American investor paid for the American railway system more than three times over in the process; but despite that fact the net advantage was to the United States. As long as we had free land; as long as population was growing by leaps and bounds; as long as our industrial plants were insufficient to supply our own needs, society chose to give the ambitious man free play and unlimited reward provided only that he produced the economic plant so much desired.

During this period of expansion, there was equal opportunity for all and the business of government was not to interfere but to assist in the development of industry. This was done at the request of business men themselves. The tariff was originally imposed for the purpose of ''fostering our infant industry'', a phrase I think the older among you will remember as a political issue not so long ago. The railroads were subsidized, sometimes by grants of money, oftener by grants of land;

some of the most valuable oil lands in the United States were granted
to assist the financing of the railroad which pushed through the South-
west. A nascent merchant marine was assisted by grants of money, or
by mail subsidies, so that our steam shipping might ply the seven seas.
Some of my friends tell me that they do not want the Government in
business. With this I agree; but I wonder whether they realize the implications of the past. For while it has been American doctrine that
the government must not go into business in competition with private
enterprises, still it has been traditional particularly in Republican administrations for business urgently to ask the government to put at
private disposal all kinds of government assistance. The same man who
tells you that he does not want to see the government interfere in business — and he means it, and has plenty of good reasons for saying so —
is the first to go to Washington and ask the government for a prohi-
bitory tariff on his product. When things get just bad enough — as they
did two years ago — he will go with equal speed to the United States
government and ask for a loan; and the Reconstruction Finance Corporation is the outcome of it. Each group has sought protection from the
government for its own special interests, without realizing that the
function of government must be to favor no small group at the expense
of its duty to protect the rights of personal freedom and of private
property of all its citizens.

In retrospect we can now see that the turn of the tide came with the
turn of the century. We were reaching our last frontier; there was no
more free land and our industrial combinations had become great un-
controlled and irresponsible units of power within the state. Clear-
sighted men saw with fear the danger that opportunity would no longer
be equal; that the growing corporation, like the feudal baron of old,
might threaten the economic freedom of individuals to earn a living.
In that hour, our antitrust laws were born. The cry was raised against
the great corporations. Theodore Roosevelt, the first great Republican
progressive, fought a Presidential campaign on the issue of "trust
busting" and talked freely about malefactors of great wealth. If the
government had a policy it was rather to turn the clock back, to destroy
the large combinations and to return to the time when every man owned
his individual small business.

This was impossible; Theodore Roosevelt, abandoning the idea of
"trust busting", was forced to work out a difference between "good"
trusts and "bad" trusts. The Supreme Court set forth the famous
"rule of reason" by which it seems to have meant that a concentration
of industrial power was permissible if the method by which it got its
power, and the use it made of that power, was reasonable.

Woodrow Wilson, elected in 1912, saw the situation more clearly.
Where Jefferson had feared the encroachment of political power on the
lives of individuals, Wilson knew that the new power was financial.
He saw, in the highly centralized economic system, the despot of the

twentieth century, on whom great masses of individuals relied for their safety and their livelihood, and whose irresponsibility and greed (if it were not controlled) would reduce them to starvation and penury. The concentration of financial power had not proceeded so far in 1912 as it has today; but it had grown far enough for Mr. Wilson to realize fully its implications. It is interesting, now, to read his speeches. What is called "radical" today (and I have reason to know whereof I speak) is mild compared to the campaign of Mr. Wilson. "No man can deny," he said, "that the lines of endeavor have more and more narrowed and stiffened; no man who knows anything about the development of industry in this country can have failed to observe that the larger kinds of credit are more and more difficult to obtain unless you obtain them upon terms of uniting your efforts with those who already control the industry of the country, and nobody can fail to observe that every man who tries to set himself up in competition with any process of manufacture which has taken place under the control of large combinations of capital will presently find himself either squeezed out or obliged to sell and allow himself to be absorbed." Had there been no World War – had Mr. Wilson been able to devote eight years to domestic instead of to international affairs – we might have had a wholly different situation at the present time. However, the then distant roar of European cannon, growing ever louder, forced him to abandon the study of this issue. The problem he saw so clearly is left with us as a legacy; and no one of us on either side of the political controversy can deny that it is a matter of grave concern to the government.

A glance at the situation today only too clearly indicates that equality of opportunity as we have known it no longer exists. Our industrial plant is built; the problem just now is whether under existing conditions it is not overbuilt. Our last frontier has long since been reached, and there is practically no more free land. More than half of our people do not live on the farms or on lands and cannot derive a living by cultivating their own property. There is no safety valve in the form of a Western prairie to which those thrown out of work by the Eastern economic machines can go for a new start. We are not able to invite the immigration from Europe to share our endless plenty. We are now providing a drab living for our own people.

Our system of constantly rising tariffs has at last reacted against us to the point of closing our Canadian frontier on the north, our European markets on the east, many of our Latin American markets to the south, and a goodly proportion of our Pacific markets on the west, through the retaliatory tariffs of those countries. It has forced many of our great industrial institutions who exported their surplus production to such countries, to establish plants in such countries within the tariff walls. This has resulted in the reduction of the operation of their American plants, and opportunity for employment.

Just as freedom to farm has ceased, so also the opportunity in business has narrowed. It still is true that men can start small enterprises, trusting to native shrewdness and ability to keep abreast of competitors; but area after area has been preempted altogether by the great corporations, and even in the fields which still have no great concerns, the small man starts under a handicap. The unfeeling statistics of the past three decades show that the independent business man is running a losing race. Perhaps he is forced to the wall; perhaps he cannot command credit; perhaps he is "squeezed out," in Mr. Wilson's words, by highly organized corporate competitors, as your corner grocery man can tell you. Recently a careful study was made of the concentration of business in the United States. It showed that our economic life was dominated by some six hundred odd corporations who controlled two-thirds of American industry. Ten million small business men divided the other third. More striking still, it appeared that if the process of concentration goes on at the same rate, at the end of another century we shall have all American industry controlled by a dozen corporations, and run by perhaps a hundred men. Put plainly, we are steering a steady course toward economic oligarchy, if we are not there already.

Clearly, all this calls for a re-appraisal of values. A mere builder of more industrial plants, a creator of more railroad systems, an organizer of more corporations, is as likely to be a danger as a help. The day of the great promoter or the financial Titan, to whom we granted anything if only he would build, or develop, is over. Our task now is not discovery or exploitation of natural resources, or necessarily producing more goods. It is the soberer, less dramatic business of administering resources and plants already in hand, of seeking to reestablish foreign markets for our surplus production, of meeting the problem of underconsumption, of adjusting production to consumption, of distributing wealth and products more equitably, of adapting existing economic organizations to the service of the people. The day of enlightened administration has come.

Just as in older times the central government was first a haven of refuge, and then a threat, so now in a closer economic system the central and ambitious financial unit is no longer a servant of national desire, but a danger. I would draw the parallel one step farther. We did not think because national government had become a threat in the 18th century that therefore we should abandon the principle of national government. Nor today should we abandon the principle of strong economic units called corporations, merely because their power is susceptible of easy abuse. In other times we dealt with the problem of an unduly ambitious central government by modifying it gradually into a constitutional democratic government. So today we are modifying and controlling our economic units.

As I see it, the task of government in its relation to business is to assist the development of an economic declaration of rights, an economic constitutional order. This is the common task of statesman and business man. It is the minimum requirement of a more permanently safe order of things. . . .

Every man has a right to life; and this means that he has also a right to make a comfortable living. He may by sloth or crime decline to exercise that right; but it may not be denied him. We have no actual famine or dearth; our industrial and agricultural mechanism can produce enough and to spare. Our government formal and informal, political and economic, owes to every one an avenue to possess himself of a portion of that plenty sufficient for his needs, through his own work.

Every man has a right to his own property; which means a right to be assured, to the fullest extent attainable, in the safety of his savings. By no other means can men carry the burdens of those parts of life which, in the nature of things afford no chance of labor; childhood, sickness, old age. In all thought of property, this right is paramount; all other property rights must yield to it. If, in accord with this principle, we must restrict the operations of the speculator, the manipulator, even the financier, I believe we must accept the restriction as needful, not to hamper individualism but to protect it.

These two requirements must be satisfied, in the main, by the individuals who claim and hold control of the great industrial and financial combinations which dominate so large a part of our industrial life. They have undertaken to be, not business men, but princes — princes of property. I am not prepared to say that the system which produces them is wrong. I am very clear that they must fearlessly and competently assume the responsibility which goes with the power. So many enlightened business men know this that the statement would be little more than a platitude, were it not for an added implication.

This implication is, briefly, that the responsible heads of finance and industry instead of acting each for himself, must work together to achieve the common end. They must, where necessary, sacrifice this or that private advantage; and in reciprocal self-denial must seek a general advantage. It is here that formal government — political government, if you choose, comes in. Whenever in the pursuit of this objective the lone wolf, the unethical competitor, the reckless promoter, the Ishmael or Insull whose hand is against every man's, declines to join in achieving an end recognized as being for the public welfare, and threatens to drag the industry back to a state of anarchy, the government may properly be asked to apply restraint. Likewise, should the group ever use its collective power contrary to the public welfare, the government must be swift to enter and protect the public interest.

The government should assume the function of economic regulation only as a last resort, to be tried only when private initiative, inspired by high responsibility, with such assistance and balance as government can give, has finally failed. As yet there has been no final failure, because there has been no attempt, and I decline to assume that this nation is unable to meet the situation.

The final term of the high contract was for liberty and the pursuit of happiness. We have learnt a great deal of both in the past century. We know that individual liberty and individual happiness mean nothing unless both are ordered in the sense that one man's meat is not another man's poison. We know that the old "rights of personal competency" — the right to read, to think, to speak, to choose and live a mode of life, must be respected at all hazards. We know that liberty to do anything which deprives others of those elemental rights is outside the protection of any compact; and that government in this regard is the maintenance of a balance, within which every individual may have a place if he will take it; in which every individual may find safety if he wishes it; in which every individual may attain such power as his ability permits, consistent with his assuming the accompanying responsibility. . . .

Faith in America, faith in our tradition of personal responsibility, faith in our institutions, faith in ourselves demands that we recognize the new terms of the old social contract. We shall fulfill them, as we fulfilled the obligation of the apparent Utopia which Jefferson imagined for us in 1776, and which Jefferson, Roosevelt and Wilson sought to bring to realization. We must do so, lest a rising tide of misery engendered by our common failure, engulf us all. But failure is not an American habit; and in the strength of great hope we must all shoulder our common load.

FIRST INAUGURAL ADDRESS
March 4, 1933

*President Roosevelt seemed to give a new spark of hope
and energy in his stirring address. His famous statement
about fear, "The only thing we have to fear is fear itself,"
his reference to the "money changers," his pledge of
leadership and call for action all make this one of the
most famous of inaugural addresses by any president.*

I am certain that my fellow Americans expect that on my induction
into the Presidency I will address them with a candor and a decision
which the present situation of our Nation impels. This is preeminently
the time to speak the truth, the whole truth, frankly and boldly. Nor
need we shrink from honestly facing conditions in our country today.
This great Nation will endure as it has endured, will revive and will
prosper. So, first of all, let me assert my firm belief that the only thing
we have to fear is fear itself—nameless, unreasoning, unjustified terror which paralyzes needed efforts to convert retreat into advance. In
every dark hour of our national life a leadership of frankness and vigor
has met with that understanding and support of the people themselves
which is essential to victory. I am convinced that you will again give
that support to leadership in these critical days.

In such a spirit on my part and on yours we face our common difficulties. They concern, thank God, only material things. Values have
shrunken to fantastic levels; taxes have risen; our ability to pay has
fallen; government of all kinds is faced by serious curtailment of income; the means of exchange are frozen in the currents of trade; the
withered leaves of industrial enterprise lie on every side; farmers
find no markets for their produce; the savings of many years in thousands of families are gone.

More important, a host of unemployed citizens face the grim problem of existence, and an equally great number toil with little return.
Only a foolish optimist can deny the dark realities of the moment.

Yet our distress comes from no failure of substance. We are
stricken by no plague of locusts. Compared with the perils which our
fore-fathers conquered because they believed and were not afraid, we
have still much to be thankful for. Nature still offers her bounty and
human efforts have multiplied it. Plenty is at our doorstep, but a generous use of it languishes in the very sight of the supply. Primarily
this is because the rulers of the exchange of mankind's goods have
failed, through their own stubborness and their own incompetence, have
admitted their failure, and abdicated. Practices of the unscrupulous
money changers stand indicted in the court of public opinion, rejected
by the hearts and minds of men.

True they have tried, but their efforts have been cast in the pattern of an outworn tradition. Faced by failure of credit they have proposed only the lending of more money. Stripped of the lure of profit by which to induce our people to follow their false leadership, they have restored to exhortations, pleading tearfully for restored confidence. They know only the rules of a generation of self-seekers. They have no vision, and when there is no vision the people perish.

The money changers have fled from their high seats in the temple of our civilization. We may now restore that temple to the ancient truths. The measure of the restoration lies in the extent to which we apply social values more noble than mere monetary profit.

Happiness lies not in the mere possession of money; it lies in the joy of achievement, in the thrill of creative effort. The joy and moral stimulation of work no longer must be forgotten in the mad chase of evanescent profits. These dark days will be worth all they cost us if they teach us that our true destiny is not to be ministered unto but to minister to ourselves and to our fellow men.

Recognition of the falsity of material wealth as the standard of success goes hand in hand with the abandonment of the false belief that public office and high political position are to be valued only by the standards of pride of place and personal profit; and there must be an end to a conduct in banking and in business which too often has given to a sacred trust the likeness of callous and selfish wrongdoing. Small wonder that confidence languishes, for it thrives only on honesty, on honor, on the sacredness of obligations, on faithful protection, on unselfish performance; without them it can not live.

Restoration calls, however, not for changes in ethics alone. This Nation asks for action, and action now.

Our greatest primary task is to put people to work. This is no unsolvable problem if we face it wisely and courageously. It can be accomplished in part by direct recruiting by the Government itself, treating the task as we would treat the emergency of a war, but at the same time, through this employment, accomplishing greatly needed projects to stimulate and reorganize the use of our natural resources.

Hand in hand with this we must frankly recognize the overbalance of population in our industrial centers and, by engaging on a national scale in a redistribution, endeavor to provide a better use of the land for those best fitted for the land. The task can be helped by definite efforts to raise the values of agricultural products and with this the power to purchase the output of our cities. It can be helped by preventing realistically the tragedy of the growing loss through foreclosure of our small homes and our farms. It can be helped by insistence that the Federal, State, and local governments act forthwith on the demand that their cost be drastically reduced. It can be helped by the unifying of relief activities which to-day are often scattered, uneconomical, and unequal. It can be helped by national planning for and supervision of all forms of transportation and of communications and other utilities which have a definitely public character. There are many ways in which it can be helped, but it can never be helped merely by talking about it. We must act and act quickly.

Finally, in our progress toward a resumption of work we require two safeguards against a return of the evils of the old order; there must be a strict supervision of all banking and credits and investments; there must be an end to speculation with other people's money, and there must be provision for an adequate but sound currency.

There are the lines of attack. I shall presently urge upon a new Congress in special session detailed measures for their fulfillment, and I shall seek the immediate assistance of the several States.

Through this program of action we address ourselves to putting our own national house in order and making income balance outgo. Our international trade relations, though vastly important, are in point of time and necessity secondary to the establishment of a sound national economy. I favor as a practical policy the putting of first things first. I shall spare no effort to restore world trade by international economic readjustment, but the emergency at home can not wait on that accomplishment.

The basic thought that guides these specific means of national recovery is not narrowly nationalistic. It is the insistence, as a first consideration, upon the interdependence of the various elements in parts of the United States — a recognition of the old and permanently important manifestation of the American spirit of the pioneer. It is the way to recovery. It is the immediate way. It is the strongest assurance that the recovery will endure.

In the field of world policy I would dedicate this Nation to the policy of the good neighbor — the neighbor who resolutely respects himself and, because he does so, respects the rights of others — the neighbor who respects his obligations and respects the sanctity of his agreements in and with a world of neighbors.

If I read the temper of our people correctly, we now realize as we have never realized before our interdependence on each other; that we can not merely take but we must give as well; that if we are to go forward, we must move as a trained and loyal army willing to sacrifice for the good of a common discipline, because without such discipline no progress is made, no leadership becomes effective. We are, I know, ready and willing to submit our lives and property to such discipline, because it makes possible a leadership which aims at a larger good. This I propose to offer, pledging that the larger purposes will bind upon us all as a sacred obligation with a unity of duty hitherto evoked only in time of armed strife.

With this pledge taken, I assume unhesitatingly the leadership of this great army of our people dedicated to a disciplined attack upon our common problems.

Action in this image and to this end is feasible under the form of government which we have inherited from our ancestors. Our Constitution is so simple and practical that it is possible always to meet extraordinary needs by changes in emphasis and arrangement without loss of essential form. That is why our constitutional system has proved itself the most superbly enduring political mechanism the modern world has produced. It has met every stress of vast expansion of territory, of foreign wars, of bitter internal strife, of world relations.

It is to be hoped that the normal balance of executive and legislative authority may be wholly adequate to meet the unprecedented task before us. But it may be that an unprecedented demand and need for undelayed action may call for temporary departure from that normal balance of public procedure.

I am prepared under my constitutional duty to recommend the measures that a stricken nation in the midst of a stricken world may require. These measures, or such other measures as the Congress may build out of its experience and wisdom, I shall seek, within my constitutional authority, to bring to speedy adoption.

But in the event that the Congress shall fail to take one of these two courses, and in the event that the national emergency is still critical, I shall not evade the clear course of duty that will then confront me, I shall ask the Congress for the one remaining instrument to meet the crisis — broad Executive power to wage a war against the emergency, as great as the power that would be given to me if we were in fact invaded by a foreign foe.

For the trust reposed in me I will return the courage and the devotion that befit the time. I can do no less.

We face the arduous days that lie before us in the warm courage of the national unity; with the clear consciousness of seeking old and precious moral values; with the clean satisfaction that comes from the stern performance of duty by old and young alike. We aim at the assurance of a rounded and permanent national life.

We do not distrust the future of essential democracy. The people of the United States have not failed. In their need they have registered a mandate that they want direct, vigorous action. They have asked for discipline and direction under leadership. They have made me the present instrument of their wishes. In the spirit of the gift I take it.

In this dedication of a Nation we humbly ask the blessing of God. May He protect each and every one of us. May He guide me in the days to come.

FIRST PRESS CONFERENCE
March 8, 1933

*The President reinstituted the press conference and was
a master in handling reporters and their questions. His
friendly, easy manner, his use of humor, and his use of
"off the record" references are illustrated in his first
meeting with the press.*

THE PRESIDENT: It is very good to see you all and my hope is
that these conferences are going to be merely enlarged editions of the
kind of very delightful family conferences I have been holding in Albany
for the last four years.

I am told that what I am about to do will become impossible, but I
am going to try it. We are not going to have any more written questions
and of course while I cannot answer seventy-five or a hundred questions because I simply haven't got the physical time, I see no reason
why I should not talk to you ladies and gentlemen off the record just the
way I have been doing in Albany and the way I used to do it in the Navy
Department down here. Quite a number of you, I am glad to see, date
back to the days of the previous existence which I led in Washington.

(Interruption — "These two boys are off for Arizona." John
and Franklin Roosevelt saying "good-bye.)"

And so I think we will discontinue the practice of compelling
the submitting of questions in writing before the conference in order to
get an answer. There will be a great many questions, of course, that
I won't answer, either because they are "if" questions — and I never
answer them — and Brother Stephenson will tell you what an "if"
question is —

MR. STEPHENSON: I ask forty of them a day.

THE PRESIDENT: And the others of course are the questions
which for various reasons I don't want to discuss or I am not ready to
discuss or I don't know anything about. There will be a great many
questions you will ask about that I don't know enough about to answer.

Then, in regard to news announcements, Steve and I thought that it
was best that street news for use out of here should be always without
direct quotations. In other words, I don't want to be directly quoted,
with the exception that direct quotations will be given out by Steve in
writing. Of course that makes that perfectly clear.

Then there are two other matters we will talk about: The first is "background information," which means material which can be used by all of you on your own authority and responsibility and must not be attributed to the White House, because I don't want to have to revive the Ananias Club.

Then the second thing is the "off the record" information which means, of course, confidential information which is given only to those who attend the conference. Now there is one thing I want to say right now on which I think you will go along with me. I want to ask you not to repeat this "off the record" confidential information either to your own editors or associates who are not here because there is always the danger that while you people may not violate the rule, somebody may forget to say. "This is off the record and confidential," and the other party may use it in a story. That is to say, it is not to be used and not to be told to those fellows who happen not to come around to the conference. In other words, this is only for those present.

Now, as to news, I don't think there is any. (Laughter)

Steve reminds me that I have just signed the application for Associate Membership in the Press Club, which I am very happy to do.

Q: Will you go to Congress or send your message?

THE PRESIDENT: Send it.

Q: When will it be available here for us?

THE PRESIDENT: Judging by the fact that I haven't started to write it, I should say at the very last minute possible. I shall let you have it as soon as I can. Of course it will be for release when transmitted. I doubt very much if you will get it very much more than half an hour before it is taken to the Capitol.

Q: Will it be brief?

THE PRESIDENT: The situation demands brevity.

Q: On the Hill they say you only recommend emergency stuff and that Congress will possibly adjourn next Monday or earlier and reconvene a short time after and take up permanent stuff as well as your complete program. Is that your idea of it?

THE PRESIDENT: I hope I can put it this way – and this comes under the second category – "background information" and "not off the record" because there is no reason why you should not use it in writing your stories. The general thought at the present time is that it is absolutely impossible by tomorrow to draft any complete or permanent legislation either on banking or on budget balancing or on anything else, because the situation, as you all know, is changing very much from day to day, so much so that if I were to ask for any specific and detailed legislation it might be that the details will have to be changed by a week from today and therefore it is necessary — I think you can make a pretty good guess — that I shall have to ask for fairly broad powers in regard to banking — such powers that would make it possible to meet the changing situation from day to day in different parts of the country. We cannot write a permanent banking act for the nation in three days. That is about the size of it.

Q: Do you favor national scrip or scrip issued by clearing houses?

THE PRESIDENT: Well, there again you are getting down to details and a very good illustration of why you cannot ask for too detailed legislation. About Monday, the day before yesterday, a very, very wide use of scrip seemed necessary and by last night it looked possible to avoid such a general use of scrip. But it does not mean that scrip will be eliminated by any means. Scrip may be used in many localities pending the working out of a sounder plan and more permanent plan to get additional currency into use. Now, I can't tell you any more about that, because we are still working on the details, but essentially it means an addition to the available currency.

Q: Could you comment on the report that no additional legislation is needed for the printing of additional currency; that a rider attached to the Home Loan Bank Bill provides for expansion to the extent of at least one and a half billion and that these Federal Reserve Bank notes are already being printed?

THE PRESIDENT: Frankly I don't know. I am inclined to think — and this answer is off the record because it is just a thought on my part — that separate legislation ought to be given on that instead of relying on some obscure clause in the Home Loan Bill. In other words, we want everything out on the table.

Q: You mentioned in your greetings to the Governors on Monday that you favored a unified banking system. Is that in your emergency plan?

THE PRESIDENT: That wasn't quite the way I put it to them. What I said to them was that it was necessary to treat the state and national banks the same way in this emergency so there would not be two different classes of banks in this country, and the other thing I said was to try to avoid forty-eight different plans of putting this into effect.

Q: Do I understand you are going to keep hold of this banking situation until permanent legislation is enacted?

THE PRESIDENT: Off the record answer, yes. . . .

Q: Shall we get ready to revive the term of "Controlled inflation?"

THE PRESIDENT: I wish somebody would invent a new term. I don't know what it is.

Q: May I ask if the long-time settlement of the banking situation is inter-meshed with the world economic conference?

THE PRESIDENT: I should say on that— background information — so far as banks go within the United States, no. So far as international exchange goes, yes. I think that is the easiest way of putting it. In other words, the opening of banks and the maintaining of banks once they are opened is not connected with the World Economic Conference.

Q: In your inaugural address, in which you only touched upon things, you said you are for sound and adequate —

THE PRESIDENT: I put it the other way around. I said "adequate but sound."

Q: Now that you have more time, can you define what that is?

THE PRESIDENT: No. In other words — and I should call this "off the record" information — you cannot define the thing too closely one way or the other. On Friday afternoon last we undoubtedly didn't have adequate currency. No question about that. There wasn't enough circulating money to go around.

Q: I believe that. (Laughter).

THE PRESIDENT: We hope that when the banks reopen a great deal of the currency that was withdrawn for one purpose or another will find its way back. We have got to provide an adequate currency. Last Friday we would have had to provide it in the form of scrip and probably some additional issues of Federal Bank notes. If things go along as we hope they will, the use of scrip can be very greatly curtailed and the amounts of new Federal Bank issues we hope can be also limited to a very great extent. In other words, what you are coming to now really is a managed currency, the adequateness of which will depend on the conditions of the moment. It may expand one week and it may contract another week. That part is all off the record.

Q: Can we use that part — managed?

THE PRESIDENT: No, I think not.
Q: That is a pretty good substitute for "controlled."

THE PRESIDENT: Go and ask [Secretary of the Treasury] Will Woodin about it.

Q: He's too busy.
Q: Now you came down to adequacy, but you haven't defined what you think is sound, or don't you want to define that now?

THE PRESIDENT: I don't want to define "sound" now. In other words, in its essence — this is entirely off the record — in its essence we must not put the Government any further in debt. Now, the real mark of delineation between sound and unsound is when the government starts to pay its bills by starting printing presses. That is about the size of it. . . .

FIRST FIRESIDE CHAT
March 12, 1933

*The President was to use "fireside chats," delivered over
the radio from the White House, or, at times after 1941,
from the Library at Hyde Park, to explain his policies in
simple terms and to ask the American people to support
them. The response to this particular address was extremely positive. By March 15, half the banks of the country,
including those with 90 percent of the deposits, reopened,
while depositers returned over a billion dollars in currency
to the banks in the next two weeks.*

I want to talk for a few minutes with the people of the United
States about banking — with the comparatively few who understand the
mechanics of banking but more particularly with the overwhelming
majority who use banks for the making of deposits and the drawing of
checks. I want to tell you what has been done in the last few days, why
it was done, and what the next steps are going to be. I reconize that
the many proclamations from State capitols and from Washington, the
legislation, the Treasury regulations, etc., couched for the most part
in banking and legal terms, should be explained for the benefit of the
average citizen. I owe this in particular because of the fortitude and
good temper with which everybody has accepted the inconvenience and
hardships of the banking holiday. I know that when you understand what
we in Washington have been about I shall continue to have your cooperation as fully as I have had your sympathy and help during the past
week.

First of all, let me state the simple fact that when you deposit
money in a bank the bank does not put the money into a safe deposit
vault. It invests your money in many different forms of credit — bonds,
commercial paper, mortgages and many other kinds of loans. In
other words, the bank puts your money to work to keep the wheels of
industry and of agriculture turning around. A comparatively small part
of the money you put into the bank is kept in currency—an amount which
in normal times is wholly sufficient to cover the cash needs of the
average citizen. In other words, the total amount of all the currency
in the country is only a small fraction of the total deposits in all of the
banks.

What, then, happened during the last few days of February and the
first few days of March? Because of undermined confidence on the part
of the public, there was a general rush by a large portion of our population to turn bank deposits into currency or gold — a rush so great
that the soundest banks could not get enough currency to meet the demand. The reason for this was that on the spur of the moment it was,
of course, impossible to sell perfectly sound assets of a bank and con-

vert them into cash except at panic prices far below their real value.

By the afternoon of March 3d scarcely a bank in the country was open to do business. Proclamations temporarily closing them in whole or in part had been issued by the Governors in almost all the States.

It was then that I issued the proclamation providing for the nationwide bank holiday, and this was the first step in the Government's reconstruction of our financial and economic fabric.

The second step was the legislation promptly and patriotically passed by the Congress confirming my proclamation and broadening my powers so that it became possible in view of the requirement of time to extend the holiday and lift the ban of that holiday gradually. This law also gave authority to develop a program of rehabilitation of our banking facilities. I want to tell our citizens in every part of the Nation that the national Congress — Republicans and Democrats alike — showed by this action a devotion to public welfare and a realization of the emergency and the necessity for speed that it is difficult to match in our history.

The third stage has been the series of regulations permitting the banks to continue their functions to take care of the distribution of food and household necessities and the payment of payrolls.

This bank holiday, while resulting in many cases in great inconvenience, is affording us the opportunity to supply the currency necessary to meet the situation. No sound bank is a dollar worse off than it was when it closed its doors last Monday. Neither is any bank which may turn out not to be in a position for immediate opening. The new law allows the twelve Federal Reserve Banks to issue additional currency on good assets and thus the banks which reopen will be able to meet every legitimate call. The new currency is being sent out by the Bureau of Engraving and Printing in large volume to every part of the country. It is sound currency because it is backed by actual, good assets.

A question you will ask is this: why are all the banks not to be reopened at the same time? The answer is simple. Your Government does not intend that the history of the past few years shall be repeated. We do not want and will not have another epidemic of bank failures.

As a result, we start tomorrow, Monday, with the opening of banks in the twelve Federal Reserve Bank cities — those banks which on first examination by the Treasury have already been found to be all right. This will be followed on Tuesday by the resumption of all their functions by banks already found to be sound in cities where there are recognized clearing houses. That means about 250 cities of the United States.

On Wednesday and succeeding days banks in smaller places all through the country will resume business, subject, of course, to the Government's physical ability to complete its survey. It is necessary that the reopening of banks be extended over a period in order to permit the banks to make applications for necessary loans, to obtain currency needed to meet their requirements and to enable the Government to make common sense checkups.

Let me make it clear to you that if your bank does not open the first day you are by no means justified in believing that it will not open. A bank that opens on one of the subsequent days is in exactly the same status as the bank that opens tomorrow.

I know that many people are worrying about State banks not members of the Federal Reserve System. These banks can and will receive assistance from member banks and from the Reconstruction Finance Corporation. These State banks are following the same course as the National banks except that they get their licenses to resume business from the State authorities, and these authorities have been asked by the Secretary of the Treasury to permit their good banks to open up on the same schedule as the national banks. I am confident that the State Banking Departments will be as careful as the national Government in the policy relating to the opening of banks and will follow the same broad policy.

It is possible that when the banks resume a very few people who have not recovered from their fear may again begin withdrawals. Let me make it clear that the banks will take care of all needs — and it is my belief that hoarding during the past week has become an exceedingly unfashionable pastime. It needs no prophet to tell you that when the people find that they can get their money — that they can get it when they want it for all legitimate purposes — the phantom of fear will soon be laid. People will again be glad to have their money where it will be safely taken care of and where they can use it conveniently at any time. I can assure you that it is safer to keep your money in a reopened bank than under the mattress.

The success of our whole great national program depends, of course, upon the cooperation of the public — on its intelligent support and use of a reliable system.

Remember that the essential accomplishment of the new legislation is that it makes it possible for banks more readily to convert their assets into cash than was the case before. More liberal provision has been made for banks to borrow on these assets at the Reserve Banks and more liberal provision has also been made for issuing currency on the security of these good assets. This currency is not fiat currency. It is issued only on adequate security, and every good bank has an abudance of such security.

One more point before I close. There will be, of course, some banks unable to reopen without being reorganized. The new law allows the Government to assist in making their reorganizations quickly and effectively and even allows the Government to subscribe to at least a part of new capital which may be required.

I hope you can see from this elemental recital of what your Government is doing that there is nothing complex, or radical, in the process.

We had a bad banking situation. Some of our bankers had shown themselves either incompetent or dishonest in their handling of the people's funds. They had used the money entrusted to them in speculations and unwise loans. This was, of course, not true in the vast majority of our banks, but it was true in enough of them to shock the people for a time into a sense of insecurity and to put them into a frame of mind where they did not differentiate, but seemed to assume that the acts of a comparative few had tainted them all. It was the Government's job to straighten out this situation and do it as quickly as possible. And the job is being performed.

I do not promise you that every bank will be reopened or that individual losses will not be suffered, but there will be no losses that possibly could be avoided; and there would have been more and greater losses had we continued to drift. I can even promise you salvation for some at least of the sorely pressed banks. We shall be engaged not merely in reopening sound banks but in the creation of sound banks through reorganization.

It has been wonderful to me to catch the note of confidence from all over the country. I can never be sufficiently grateful to the people for the loyal support they have given me in their acceptance of the judgment that has dictated our course, even though all our processes may not have seemed clear to them.

After all, there is an element in the readjustment of our financial system more important than currency, more important than gold, and that is the confidence of the people. Confidence and courage are the essentials of success in carrying out our plan. You people must have faith, you must not be stampeded by rumors or guesses. Let us unite in banishing fear. We have provided the machinery to restore our financial system; it is up to you to support and make it work.

It is your problem no less than it is mine. Together we cannot fail.

SECOND FIRESIDE CHAT
May 7, 1933

The President again went to the radio to explain to the American people the first pieces of legislature of the "Hundred Days," and to explain the action, announced in April, of going off the gold standard.

On a Sunday night a week after my inauguration I used the radio to tell you about the banking crisis and the measures we were taking to meet it. I think that in that way I made clear to the country various facts that might otherwise have been misunderstood and in general provided a means of understanding which did much to restore confidence.

Tonight, eight weeks later, I come for the second time to give you my report; in the same spirit and by the same means to tell you about what we have been doing and what we are planning to do.

Two months ago we were facing serious problems. The country was dying by inches. It was dying because trade and commerce had declined to dangerously low levels; prices for basic commodities were such as to destroy the value of the assets of national institutions such as banks, savings banks, insurance companies, and others. These institutions, because of their great needs, were foreclosing mortgages, calling loans, refusing credit. Thus there was actually in process of destruction the property of millions of people who had borrowed money on that property in terms of dollars which had had an entirely different value from the level of March, 1933. That situation in that crisis did not call for any complicated consideration of economic panaceas or fancy plans. We were faced by a condition and not a theory.

There were just two alternatives: The first was to allow the foreclosures to continue, credit to be withheld and money to go into hiding, thus forcing liquidation and bankruptcy of banks, railroads and insurance companies and a recapitalizing of all business and all property on a lower level. This alternative meant a continuation of what is loosely called "deflation," the net result of which would have been extraordinary hardships on all property owners and, incidentally, extraordinary hardships on all persons working for wages through an increase in unemployment and a further reduction of the wage scale.

It is easy to see that the result of this course would have not only economic effects of a very serious nature, but social results that might bring incalculable harm. Even before I was inaugurated I came to the conclusion that such a policy was too much to ask the American people to bear. It involved not only a further loss of homes, farms, savings and wages, but also a loss of spiritual values – the loss of that sense of security for the present and the future so necessary to the peace and contentment of the individual and of his family. When you destroy these things you will find it difficult to establish confidence of any sort in the future. It was clear that mere appeals from Washington for confidence and the mere lending of more money to shaky institutions could not stop this downward course. A prompt program applied as quickly as possible seemed to me not only justified but imperative to our national security. The Congress, and when I say Congress I mean the members of both political parties, fully understood this and gave me generous and intelligent support. The members of Congress realized that the methods of normal times had to be replaced in the emergency by measures which were suited to the serious and pressing requirements of the moment. There was no actual surrender of power. Congress still retained its constitutional authority, and no one has the slightest desire to change the balance of these powers. The function of Congress is to decide what has to be done and to select the appropriate agency to carry out its will. To this policy it has strictly adhered. The only thing that has been happening has been to designate the President as the agency to carry out certain of the purposes of the Congress. This was constitutional and in keeping with the past American tradition.

The legislation which has been passed or is in the process of enactment can properly be considered as part of a well-grounded plan.

First, we are giving opportunity of employment to one-quarter of a million of the unemployed, especially the young men who have dependents, to go into the forestry and flood-prevention work. This is a big task because it means feeding, clothing and caring for nearly twice as many men as we have in the regular army itself. In creating this civilian conservation corps we are killing two birds with one stone. We are clearly enhancing the value of our natural resources, and we are relieving an appreciable amount of actual distress. This great group of men has entered upon its work on a purely voluntary basis; no military training is involved and we are conserving not only our natural resources, but our human resources. One of the great values to this work is the fact that it is direct and requires the intervention of very little machinery.

Second, I have requested the Congress and have secured action upon a proposal to put the great properties owned by our Government at Muscle Shoals to work after long years of wasteful inaction, and with this a broad plan for the improvement of a vast area in the Tennessee Valley. It will add to the comfort and happiness of hundreds of thousands of people and the incident benefits will reach the entire Nation.

Next, the Congress is about to pass legislation that will greatly ease the mortgage distress among the farmers and the home owners of the Nation, by providing for the easing of the burden of debt now bearing so heavily upon millions of our people.

Our next step in seeking immediate relief is a grant of half a billion dollars to help the States, counties and municipalities in their duty to care for those who need direct and immediate relief.

The Congress also passed legislation authorizing the sale of beer in such States as desired it. This has already resulted in considerable reemployment and incidentally has provided much-needed tax revenue.

We are planning to ask the Congress for legislation to enable the Government to undertake public works, thus stimulating directly and indirectly the employment of many others in well-considered projects.

Further legislation has been taken up which goes much more fundamentally into our economic problems. The Farm Relief Bill seeks by the use of several methods, alone or together, to bring about an increased return to farmers for their major farm products, seeking at the same time to prevent in the days to come disastrous over-production which so often in the past has kept farm commodity prices far below a reasonable return. This measure provides wide powers for emergencies. The extent of its use will depend entirely upon what the future has in store.

Well-considered and conservative measures will likewise be proposed which will attempt to give to the industrial workers of the country a more fair wage return, prevent cut-throat competition and unduly long hours for labor, and at the same time encourage each industry to prevent overproduction.

Our Railroad Bill falls into the same class because it seeks to provide and make certain definite planning by the railroads themselves, with the assistance of the Government, to eliminate the duplication and waste that is now resulting in railroad receiverships and continuing operating deficits.

I am certain that the people of this country understand and approve the broad purposes behind these new governmental policies relating to agriculture and industry and transportation. We found ourselves faced with more agricultural products than we could possibly consume ourselves, and with surpluses which other Nations did not have the cash to buy from us except at prices ruinously low. We found our factories able to turn out more goods than we could possibly consume, and at the same time we were faced with a falling export demand. We found ourselves with more facilities to transport goods and crops than there were goods and crops to be transported. All of this has been caused in large part by a complete lack of planning and a complete failure to understand the danger signals that have been flying ever since the close of the World War. The people of this country have been erroneously encouraged to believe that they could keep on increasing the output of farm and factory indefinitely and that some magician would find ways and means for that increased output to be consumed with reasonable profit to the producer.

Today we have reason to believe that things are a little better than they were two months ago. Industry has picked up, railroads are carrying more freight, farm prices are better, but I am not going to indulge in issuing proclamations of over-enthusiastic assurance. We cannot ballyhoo ourselves back to prosperity. I am going to be honest at all times with the people of the country. I do not want the people of this country to take the foolish course of letting this improvement come back on another speculative wave. I do not want the people to believe that because of unjustified optimism we can resume the ruinous practice of increasing our crop output and our factory output in the hope that a kind Providence will find buyers at high prices. Such a course may bring us immediate and false prosperity but it will be the kind of prosperity that will lead us into another tailspin.

It is wholly wrong to call the measures that we have taken Governmental control of farming, industry, and transportaton. It is rather a partnership between Government and farming and industry and transportation, not partnership in profits, for the profits still go to citizens, but rather a partnership in planning, and a partnership to see that the plans are carried out.

Let me illustrate with an example. Take the cotton-goods industry. It is probably true that 90 percent of the cotton manufacturers would agree to eliminate starvation wages, would agree to stop long hours of employment, would agree to stop child labor, would agree to prevent an overproduction that would result in unsalable surpluses. But, what good is such an agreement if the other 10 percent of cotton manufacturers pay starvation wages, require long hours, employ children in their mills and turn out burdensome surpluses? The unfair 10 percent could produce goods so cheaply that the fair 90 percent would be compelled to meet the unfair conditions. Here is where the Government comes in. Government ought to have the right and will have the right, after surveying and planning for an industry, to prevent, with the assistance of the overwhelming majority of that industry, unfair practices and to enforce this agreement by the authority of Government. The so-called antitrust laws were intended to prevent the creation of monopolies and to forbid unreasonable profits to those monopolies. That purpose of the anti-trust laws must be continued, but these laws were never intended to encourage the kind of unfair competition that results in long hours, starvation wages and overproduction.

The same principle applies to farm products and to transportation and every other field of organized private industry.

We are working toward a definite goal, which is to prevent the return of conditions which came very close to destroying what we call modern civilization. The actual accomplishment of our purpose cannot be attained in a day. Our policies are wholly within purposes for which our American Constitutional Government was established 150 years ago.

I know that the people of this country will understand this and will also understand the spirit in which we are undertaking this policy. I do not deny that we may make mistakes of procedure as we carry out the policy. I have no expectation of making a hit every time I come to bat. What I seek is the highest possible batting average, not only for myself but for the team. Theodore Roosevelt once said to me: "If I can be right 75 percent of the time I shall come up to the fullest measure of my hopes.

Much has been said of late about Federal finances and inflation, the gold standard, etc. Let me make the facts very simple and my policy very clear. In the first place, Government credit and Government currency are really one and the same thing. Behind Government bonds there is only a promise to pay. Behind Government currency we have, in addition to the promise to pay, a reserve of gold and a small reserve of silver. In this connection it is worth while remembering that in the past the Government has agreed to redeem nearly thirty billions of its debts and its currency in gold, and private corporations in this country have agreed to redeem another sixty or seventy billions of securities and mortgages in gold. The Government and private corporations were making these agreements when they knew full well that all of the gold in the United States amounted to only between three and four billions and that all of the gold in all of the world amounted to only about eleven billions.

If the holders of these promises to pay started in to demand gold the first comers would get gold for a few days and they would amount to about one-twenty-fifth of the holders of the securities and the currency. The other twenty-four people out of twenty-five, who did not happen to be at the top of the line, would be told politely that there was no more gold left. We have decided to treat all twenty-five in the same way in the interest of justice and the exercise of the constitutional powers of this Government. We have placed everyone on the same basis in order that the general good may be preserved.

Nevertheless, gold, and to a partial extent silver, are perfectly good bases for currency, and that is why I decided not to let any of the gold now in the country go out of it.

A series of conditions arose three weeks ago which very readily might have meant, first, a drain on our gold by foreign countries, and second, as a result of that, a flight of American capital, in the form of gold, out of our country. It is not exaggerating the possibility to tell you that such an occurrence might well have taken from us the major part of our gold reserve and resulted in such a further weakening of our Government and private credit as to bring on actual panic conditions and the complete stoppage of the wheels of industry.

The Administration has the definite objective of raising commodity prices to such an extent that those who have borrowed money will, on the average, be able to repay that money in the same kind of dollar which they borrowed. We do not seek to let them get such a cheap dollar that they will be able to pay back a great deal less than they borrowed. in other words, we seek to correct a wrong and not to create another wrong in the opposite direction. That is why powers are being given to the Administration to provide, if necessary, for an enlargement of credit, in order to correct the existing wrong. These powers will be used when, as, and if it may be necessary to accomplish the purpose.

Hand in hand with the domestic situation which, of course, is our first concern is the world situation, and I want to emphasize to you that the domestic situation is inevitably and deeply tied in with the conditions in all of the other Nations of the world. In other words, we can get, in all probability, a fair measure of prosperity to return in the United States, but it will not be permanent unless we get a return to prosperity all over the world.

In the conferences which we have held and are holding with the leaders of other Nations, we are seeking four great objectives: first, a general reduction of armaments and through this the removal of the fear of invasion and armed attack, and, at the same time, a reduction in armament costs, in order to help in the balancing of Government budgets and the reduction of taxation; second, a cutting down of the trade barriers, in order to restart the flow of exchange of crops and goods between Nations; third, the setting up of a stabilization of currencies, in order that trade can make contracts ahead; fourth, the reestablishment of friendly relations and greater confidence between all Nations.

Our foreign visitors these past three weeks have responded to these purposes in a very helpful way. All of the Nations have suffered alike in this great depression. They have all reached the conclusion that each can best be helped by the common action of all. It is in this spirit that our visitors have met with us and discussed our common problems. The international conference that lies before us must succeed. The future of the world demands it and we have each of us pledged ourselves to the best joint efforts to this end.

To you, the people of this country, all of us, the members of the Congress and the members of this Administration, owe a profound debt of gratitude. Throughout the depression you have been patient. You have granted us wide powers; you have encouraged us with a widespread approval of our purposes. Every ounce of strength and every resource at our command we have devoted to the end of justifying your confidence. We are encouraged to believe that a wise and sensible beginning has been made. In the present spirit of mutual confidence and mutual encouragement we go forward.

"BOMBSHELL MESSAGE" TO THE
LONDON ECONOMIC CONFERENCE
July 3, 1933

President Roosevelt had seemed to favor international economic cooperation in his earlier instructions to the American delegates to the World Economic Conference in London. But the measures of the Hundred Days had seemed to be working to achieve monetary stability at home, and to tie the dollar to foreign currencies would prevent manipulation of the gold content of the dollar to raise prices. Thus he "wrecked" the conference by his sharp criticism as shown in this message.

I would regard it as a catastrophe amounting to a world tragedy if the great Conference of Nations, called to bring about a more real and permanent financial stability and a greater prosperity to the masses of all nations, should, in advance of any serious effort to consider these broader problems, allow itself to be divereted by the proposal of a purely artificial and temporary experiment affecting the monetary excahnge of a few nations only. Such action, such diversion, shows a singular lack of proportion and a failure to remember the larger purposes for which the Economic Conference was called together.

I do not relish the thought that insistence on such action should be made an excuse for the continuance of the basic economic errors that underlie so much of the present world wide depression.

The world will not long be lulled by the specious fallacy of achieving a temporary and probably an artificial stability in foreign exchange on the part of a few large countries only.

The sound internal economic system of a nation is a greater factor in its well being than the price of its currency in changing terms of the currencies of other nations. . . .

The Conference was called to better and perhaps to cure fundamental economic ills. It must not be diverted from that effort.

THIRD FIRESIDE CHAT
July 24, 1933

In this radio broadcast the President explained the re-
covery measures which had been passed and launched the
"Blue Eagle" campaign which would be used to indicate
support for the National Industrial Recovery Act (NRA).

After the adjournment of the historical special session of the Congress five weeks ago I purposely refrained from addressing you for
two very good reasons.

First, I think that we all wanted the opportunity of a little quiet
thought to examine and assimilate in a mental picture the crowding
events of the Hundred Days which had been devoted to the starting of
the wheels of the New Deal.

Secondly, I wanted a few weeks in which to set up the new administrative organization and to see the first fruits of our careful planning.

I think it will interest you if I set forth the fundamentals of this
planning for national recovery; and this I am very certain will make it
abundantly clear to you that all of the proposals and all of the legislation since the fourth day of March have not been just a collection of
haphazard schemes, but rather the orderly component parts of a connected and logical whole.

Long before Inauguration Day I became convinced that individual effort and local effort and even disjointed Federal effort had failed and
of necessity would fail and, therefore, that a rounded leadership by
the Federal Government had become a necessity both of theory and of
fact. Such leadership, however, had its beginning in preserving and
strengthening the credit of the United States Government, because
without that no leadership was a possibility. For years the Government
had not lived within its income. The immediate task was to bring our
regular expenses within our revenues. That has been done.

It may seem inconsistent for a government to cut down its regular
expenses and at the same time to borrow and to spend billions for an
emergency. But it is not inconsistent because a large portion of the
emergency money has been paid out in the form of sound loans which
will be repaid to the Treasury over a period of years; and to cover the
rest of the emergency money we have imposed taxes to pay the interest
and the installments on that part of the debt.

So you will see that we have kept our credit good. We have built a
granite foundation in a period of confusion. That foundation of the Federal credit stands there broad and sure. It is the base of the whole recovery plan.

Then came the part of the problem that concerned the credit of the individual citizens themselves. You and I know of the banking crisis and of the great danger to the savings of our people. On March sixth every national bank was closed. One month later 90 per cent of the deposits in the national banks had been made available to the depositors. Today only about 5 per cent of the deposits in national banks are still tied up. The condition relating to State banks, while not quite so good on a percentage basis, is showing a steady reduction in the total of frozen deposits — a result much better than we had expected three months ago.

The problem of the credit of the individual was made more difficult because of another fact. The dollar was a different dollar from the one with which the average debt had been incurred. For this reason large numbers of people were actually losing possession of and title to their farms and homes. All of you know the financial steps which have been taken to correct this inequality. In addition the Home Loan Act, the Farm Loan Act and the Bankruptcy Act were passed.

It was a vital necessity to restore purchasing power by reducing the debt and interest charges upon our people, but while we were helping people to save their credit it was at the same time absolutely essential to do something about the physical needs of hundreds of thousands who were in dire straits at that very moment. Municipal and State aid were being stretched to the limit. We appropriated half a billion dollars to supplement their efforts and in addition, as you know, we have put 300,000 young men into practical and useful work in our forests and to prevent flood and soil erosion. The wages they earn are going in greater part to the support of the nearly one million people who constitute their families.

In this same classification we can properly place the great public works program running to a total of over three billion dollars — to be used for highways and ships and flood prevention and inland navigation and thousands of self-sustaining State and municipal improvements. Two points should be made clear in the allotting and administration of these projects: first, we are using the utmost care to choose labor-creating, quick-acting, useful projects, avoiding the smell of the pork barrel; and second, we are hoping that at least half of the money will come back to the Government from projects which will pay for themselves over a period of years.

Thus far I have spoken primarily of the foundation stones — the measures that were necessary to reestablish credit and to head people in the opposite direction by preventing distress and providing as much work as possible through governmental agencies. Now I come to the links which will build us a more lasting prosperity. I have said that we cannot attain that in a Nation half boom and half broke. If all of our people have work and fair wages and fair profits, they can buy the products of their neighbors, and business is good. But if you take away the wages and the profits of half of them, business is only half as good. It does not help much if the fortunate half is very prosperous; the best way is for everybody to be reasonably prosperous.

For many years the two great barriers to a normal prosperity have been low farm prices and the creeping paralysis of unemployment. These factors have cut the purchasing power of the country in half. I promised action. Congress did its part when it passed the Farm and the Industrial Recovery Acts. Today we are putting these two Acts to work and they will work if people understand their plain objectives.

First, the Farm Act: It is based on the fact that the purchasing power of nearly half of our population depends on adequate prices for farm products. We have been producing more of some crops than we consume or can sell in a depressed world market. The cure is not to produce so much. Without our help the farmers cannot get together and cut production, and the Farm Bill gives them a method of bringing their production down to a reasonable level and of obtaining reasonable prices for their crops. I have clearly stated that this method is in a sense experimental, but so far as we have gone we have reason to believe that it will produce good results.

It is obvious that if we can greatly increase the purchasing power of the tens of millions of our people who make a living from farming and the distribution of farm crops, we shall greatly increase the consumption of those goods which are turned out by industry.

That brings me to the final step — bringing back industry along sound lines.

Last Autumn, on several occasions, I expressed my faith that we can make possible by democratic self-discipline in industry general increases in wages and shortening of hours sufficient to enable industry to pay its own workers enough to let those workers buy and use the things that their labor produces. This can be done only if we permit and encourage cooperative action in industry, because it is obvious that without united action a few selfish men in each competitive group will pay starvation wages and insist on long hours of work. Others in that group must either follow suit or close up shop. We have seen the result of action of that kind in the continuing descent into the economic hell of the past four years.

There is a clear way to reverse that process: If all employers in each competitve group agree to pay their workers the same wages — reasonable wages — and require the same hours — reasonable hours — then higher wages and shorter hours will hurt no employer. Moreover, such action is better for the employer than unemployment and low wages, because it makes more buyers for his product. That is the simple idea which is the very heart of the Industrial Recovery Act.

On the basis of this simple principle of everybody doing things together, we are starting out on this nationwide attack on unemployment. It will succeed if our people understand it — in the big industries, in the little shops, in the great cities and in the small villages. There is nothing complicated about it and there is nothing particularly new in the principle. It goes back to the basic idea of society and of the Nation itself that people acting in a group can accomplish things which no individual acting alone could even hope to bring about.

Here is an example. In the Cotton Textile Code and in other agreements already signed, child labor has been abolished. That makes me personally happier than any other one thing with which I have been connected since I came to Washington. In the textile industry — an industry which came to me spontaneously and with a splendid cooperation as soon as the Recovery Act was signed — child labor was an old evil. But no employer acting alone was able to wipe it out. If one employer tried it, or if one State tried it, the costs of operation rose so high that it was impossible to compete with the employers of States which had failed to act. The moment the Recovery Act was passed, this monstrous thing which neither opinion nor law could reach through years of effort went out in a flash. As a British editorial put it, we did more under a Code in one day than they in England had been able to do under the common law in eighty-five years of effort. I use this incident, my friends, not to boast of what has already been done but to point the way to you for even greater cooperative efforts this summer and autumn.

We are not going through another winter like the last. I doubt if ever any people so bravely and cheerfully endured a season half so bitter. We cannot ask America to continue to face such needless hardships. It is time for courageous action, and the Recovery Bill gives us the means to conquer unemployment with exactly the same weapon that we have used to strike down child labor.

The proposition is simply this:

If all employers will act together to shorten hours and raise wages we can put people back to work. No employer will suffer, because the relative level of competitive cost will advance by the same amount for all. But if any considerable group should lag or shirk, this great opportunity will pass us by and we shall go into another desperate winter. This must not happen.

We have sent out to all employers an agreement which is the result of weeks of consultation. This agreement checks against the voluntary codes of nearly all the large industries which have already been submitted. This blanket agreement carries the unanimous approval of the three boards which I have appointed to advise in this, boards representing the great leaders in labor, in industry, and in social service. The agreement has already brought a flood of approval from every State, and from so wide a cross-section of the common calling of industry that I know it is fair for all. It is a plan – deliberate, reasonable and just – intended to put into effect at once the most important of the broad principles which are being established, industry by industry, through codes. Naturally, it takes a good deal of organizing and a great many hearings and many months, to get these codes perfected and signed, and we cannot wait for all of them to go through. The blanket agreements, however, which I am sending to every employer will start the wheels turning now, and not six months from now.

There are, of course, men, a few men, who might thwart this great common purpose by seeking selfish advantage. There are adequate penalties in the law, but I am now asking the cooperation that comes from opinion and from conscience. These are the only instruments we shall use in this great summer offensive against unemployment. But we shall use them to the limit to protect the willing from the laggard and to make the plan succeed.

In war, in the gloom of night attack, soldiers wear a bright badge on their shoulders to be sure that comrades do not fire on comrades. On that principle, those who cooperate in this program must know each other at a glance. That is why we have provided a badge of honor for this purpose, a simple design with a legend, "We do our part," and I ask that all those who join with me shall display that badge prominently. It is essential to our purpose.

Already all the great, basic industries have come forward willingly with proposed codes, and in these codes they accept the principles leading to mass reemployment. But, important as is this heartening demonstration, the richest field for results is among the small employers, those whose contribution will be to give new work for from one to ten people. These smaller employers are indeed a vital part of the backbone of the country, and the success of our plan lies largely in their hands.

Already the telegrams and letters are pouring into the White House – messages from employers who ask that their names be placed on this special Roll of Honor. They represent great corporations and companies and partnerships and individuals. I ask that even before the dates set in the agreements which we have sent out, the employers of the country who have not already done so – the big fellows and the little fellows – shall at once write or telegraph to me personally at the White House, expressing their intentions of going through with the plan. And it is my purpose to keep posted in the post office of every town, a Roll of Honor of all those who join with me.

I want to take this occasion to say to the twenty-four Governors who are now in conference in San Francisco, that nothing thus far has helped in strengthening this great movement more than their resolutions adopted at the very outset of their meeting, giving this plan their instant and unanimous approval, and pledging to support it in their States.

To the men and women whose lives have been darkened by the fact or the fear of unemployment, I am justified in saying a word of encouragement because the codes and the agreements already approved, or about to be passed upon, prove that the plan does raise wages, and that it does put people back to work. You can look on every employer who adopts the plan as one who is doing his part, and those employers deserve well of everyone who works for a living. It will be clear to you, as it is to me, that while the shirking employer may undersell his competitor, the saving he thus makes is made at the expense of his country's welfare.

While we are making this great common effort there should be no discord and dispute. This is no time to cavil or to question the standard set by this universal agreement. It is time for patience and understanding and cooperation. The workers of this country have rights under this law which cannot be taken from them, and nobody will be permitted to whittle them away but, on the other hand, no aggression is now necessary to attain those rights. The whole country will be united to get them for you. The principle that applies to the employers applies to the workers as well, and I ask you workers to cooperate in the same spirit.

When Andrew Jackson, "Old Hickory," died, someone asked, "Will he go to Heaven?" and the answer was, "He will if he wants to." If I am asked whether the American people will pull themselves out of this depression, I answer, "They will if they want to." The essence of the plan is a universal limitation of hours of work per week for any individual by common consent, and a universal payment of wages above a minimum, also by common consent. I cannot guarantee the success of this nation-wide plan, but the people of this country can guarantee its success. I have no faith in "curealls" but I believe that we can greatly influence economic forces. I have no sympathy with the professional economists who insist that things must run their course and that human agencies can have no influence on economic ills. One reason is that I happen to know that professional economists have changed their definition of economic laws every five or ten years for a very long time, but I do have faith, and retain faith, in the strength of the common purpose, and in the strength of unified action taken by the American people.

That is why I am describing to you the simple purposes and the solid foundations upon which our program of recovery is built. That is why I am asking the employers of the Nation to sign this common covenant with me — to sign it in the name of patriotism and humanity. That is why I am asking the workers to go along with us in a spirit of understanding and of helpfulness.

SECOND INAUGURAL ADDRESS
January 20, 1937

A confident President Roosevelt, after his landslide victory the previous November, pledged that his second term in office would meet the challenge posed by "one-third of a nation ill-housed, ill-clad, ill-nourished."

When four years ago we met to inaugurate a President, the Republic, single-minded in anxiety, stood in spirit here. We dedicated ourselves to the fulfillment of a vision — to speed the time when there would be for all the people that security and peace essential to the pursuit of happiness. We of the Republic pledged ourselves to drive from the temple of our ancient faith those who had profaned it; to end by action, tireless and unafraid, the stagnation and despair of that day. We did those first things first.

Our covenant with ourselves did not stop there. Instinctively we recognized a deeper need — the need to find through government the instrument of our united purpose to solve for the individual the ever-rising problems of a complex civilization. Repeated attempts at their solution without the aid of government had left us baffled and bewildered. For, without that aid, we had been unable to create those moral controls over the services of science which are necessary to make science a useful servant instead of a ruthless master of mankind. To do this we knew that we must find practical controls over blind economic forces and blindly selfish men.

We of the Republic sensed the truth that democratic government has innate capacity to protect its people against disasters once considered inevitable, to solve problems once considered unsolvable. We would not admit that we could not find a way to master economic epidemics just as, after centuries of fatalistic suffering, we had found a way to master epidemics of disease. We refused to leave the problems of our common welfare to be solved by the winds of chance and the hurricanes of disaster.

In this we Americans were discovering no wholly new truth; we were writing a new chapter in our book of self-government.

This year marks the one hundred and fiftieth anniversary of the Constitutional Convention which made us a nation. At that Convention our forefathers found the way out of the chaos which followed the Revolutionary War; they created a strong government with powers of united action sufficient then and now to solve problems utterly beyond individual or local solution. A century and a half ago they established the Federal Government in order to promote the general welfare and secure the blessings of liberty to the American people.

Today we invoke those same powers of government to achieve the same objectives.

Four years of new experience have not belied our historic instinct. They hold out the clear hope that government within communities, government within the separate States, and government of the United States can do the things the times require, without yielding its democracy. Our tasks in the last four years did not force democracy to take a holiday.

Nearly all of us recognize that as intricacies of human relationships increase, so power to govern them also must increase — power to stop evil; power to do good. The essential democracy of our Nation and the safety of our people depend not upon the absence of power, but upon lodging it with those whom the people can change or continue at stated intervals through an honest and free system of elections. The Constitution of 1787 did not make our democracy impotent.

In fact, in these last four years, we have made the exercise of all power more democratic; for we have begun to bring private autocratic powers into their proper subordination to the public's government. The legend that they were invincible — above and beyond the processes of a democracy — has been shattered. They have been challenged and beaten.

Our progress out of the depression is obvious. But that is not all that you and I mean by the new order of things. Our pledge was not merely to do a patchwork job with secondhand materials. By using the new materials of social justice we have undertaken to erect on the old foundations a more enduring structure for the better use of future generations.

In that purpose we have been helped by achievements of mind and spirit. Old truths have been relearned; untruths have been unlearned. We have always known that heedless self-interest was bad morals; we know now that it is bad economics. Out of the collapse of a prosperity whose builders boasted their practicality has come the conviction that in the long run economic morality pays. We are beginning to wipe out the line that divides the practical from the ideal; and in so doing we are fashioning an instrument of unimagined power for the establishment of a morally better world.

This new understanding undermines the old admiration of worldly success as such. We are beginning to abandon our tolerance of the abuse of power by those who betray for profit the elementary decencies of life.

In this process evil things formerly accepted will not be so easily condoned. Hard-headedness will not so easily excuse hard-heartedness.

We are moving toward an era of good feeling. But we realize that there can be no era of good feeling save among men of good will.

For these reasons I am justified in believing that the greatest cahnge we have witnessed has been the change in the moral climate of America.

Among men of good will, science and democracy together offer an ever-richer life and ever-larger satisfaction to the individual With this change in our moral climate and our rediscovered ability to improve our economic order, we have set our feet upon the road of enduring progress.

Shall we pause now and turn our back upon the road that lies ahead? Shall we call this the promised land? Or, shall we continue on our way? For "each age is a dream that is dying, or one that is coming to birth."

Many voices are heard as we face a great decision. Comfort says, "Tarry a while." Opportunism says, "This is a good spot." Timidity asks, "How difficult is the road ahead?"

True, we have come far from the days of stagnation and despair. Vitality has been preserved. Courage and confidence have been restored. Mental and moral horizons have been extended.

But our present gains were won under the pressure of more than ordinary circumstances. Advance became imperative under the goad of fear and suffering. The times were on the side of progress.

To hold to progress today, however, is more difficult. Dulled conscience, irresponsibility, and ruthless self-interest already reappear. Such symptoms of prosperity may become portents of disaster! Prosperity already tests the persistence of our progressive purpose.

Let us ask again: Have we reached the goal of our vision of that fourth day of March 1933? Have we found our happy valley?

I see a great nation, upon a great continent, blessed with a great wealth of natural resources. Its hundred and thirty million people are at peace among themselves; they are making their country a good neighbor among the nations. I see a United States which can demonstrate that, under democratic methods of government, national wealth can be translated into a spreading volume of human comforts hitherto unknown, and the lowest standard of living can be raised far above the level of mere subsistence.

But here is the challenge to our democracy: In this nation I see tens of millions of its citizens – a sustantial part of its whole population – who at this very moment are denied the greater part of what the very lowest standards of today call the necessities of life.

I see millions of families trying to live on incomes so meager that the pall of family disaster hangs over them day by day.

I see millions whose daily lives in city and on farm continue under conditions labeled indecent by a so-called polite society half a century ago.

I see millions denied education, recreation, and the opportunity to better their lot and the lot of their children.

I see millions lacking the means to buy the products of farm and factory and by their poverty denying work and productiveness to many other millions.

I see one-third of a nation ill-housed, ill-clad, ill-nourished.

It is not in despair that I paint you that picture. I paint it for you in hope — because the Nation, seeing and understanding the injustice in it; proposes to paint it out. We are determined to make every American citizen the subject of his country's interest and concern; and we will never regard any faithful law-abiding group within our borders as superfluous. The test of our progress is not whether we add more to the abundance of those who have much; it is whether we provide enough for those who have too little.

If I know aught of the spirit and purpose of our Nation, we will not listen to Comfort, Opportunism, and Timidity. We will carry on.

Overwhelmingly, we of the Republic are men and women of good will; men and women who have more than warm hearts of dedication; men and women who have cool heads and willing hands of practical purpose as well. They will insist that every agency of popular government use effective instruments to carry out their will.

Government is competent when all who compose it work as trustees for the whole people. It can make constant progress when it keeps abreast of all the facts. It can obtain justified support and legitimate criticism when the people receive true information of all that government does.

If I know aught of the will of our people, they will demand that these conditions of effective government shall be created and maintained. They will demand a nation uncorrupted by cancers of injustice and, therefore, strong among the nations in its example of the will to peace.

Today we reconsecrate our country to long-cherished ideals in a suddenly changed civilization. In every land there are always at work forces that drive men apart and forces that draw men together. In our personal ambitions we are individualists. But in our seeking for economic and political progress as a nation, we all go up, or else we all go down, as one people.

To maintain a democracy of effort requires a vast amount of patience in dealing with differing methods, a vast amount of humility. But out of the confusion of many voices rises an understanding of dominant public need. Then political leadership can voice common ideals, and aid in their realization.

In taking again the oath of office as President of the United States, I assume the solemn obligation of leading the American people forward along the road over which they have chosen to advance.

While this duty rests upon me I shall do my utmost to speak ttheir purpose and to do their will, seeking Divine guidance to help us each and every one to give light to them that sit in darkness and to guide our feet into the way of peace.

FIRESIDE CHAT ON THE "COURT PACKING" PLAN
March 9, 1937

The President in this message tried to win public support for his Judiciary Reorganization Bill, sent to Congress on February 5. The Supreme Court had upset such New Deal measures as the NRA and the AAA, and Roosevelt had not yet had an opportunity to appoint a member to the Court.

The idea failed, and the President suffered a major setback.

My friends, last Thursday I described in detail certain economic problems which everyone admits now face the Nation. For the many messages which have come to me after that speech, and which it is physically impossible to answer individually, I take this means of saying "Thank you."

Tonight, sitting at my desk in the White House, I make my first radio report to the people in my second term of office.

I am reminded of that evening in March, four years ago, when I made my first radio report to you. We were then in the midst of the great banking crisis.

Soon after, with the authority of the Congress, we asked the Nation to turn over all of its privately held gold, dollar for dollar, to the Government of the United States.

Today's recovery proves how right that policy was.

But when, almost two years later, it came before the Supreme Court, its constitutionality was upheld only by a five-to-four vote. The change of one vote would have thrown all the affairs of this great Nation back into hopeless chaos. In effect, four Justices ruled that the right under a private contract to exact a pound of flesh was more sacred than the main objectives of the Constitution to establish an enduring Nation.

In 1933 you and I knew that we must never let our economic system get completely out of joint again — that we could not afford to take the risk of another great depression.

We also became convinced that the only way to avoid a repetition of those dark days was to have a government with power to prevent and to cure the abuses and the inequalities which had thrown that system out of joint.

We then began a program of remedying those abuses and inequalities — to give balance and stability to our economic system — to make it bomb-proof against the causes of 1929.

Today we are only part-way through that program – and recovery is speeding up to a point where the dangers of 1929 are again becoming possible, not this week or month perhaps, but within a year or two.

National laws are needed to complete that program. Individual or local or state effort alone cannot protect us in 1937 any better than ten years ago.

It will take time – and plenty of time – to work out our remedies administratively even after legislation is passed. To complete our program of protection in time, therefore, we cannot delay one moment in making certain that our National Government has power to carry through.

Four years ago action did not come until the eleventh hour. It was almost too late.

If we learned anything from the depression we will not allow ourselves to run around in new circles of futile discussion and debate, always postponing the day of decision.

The American people have learned from the depression. For in the last three national elections an overwhelming majority of them voted a mandate that the Congress and the President begin the task of providing that protection – not after long years of debate, but now.

The Courts, however, have cast doubts on the ability of the elected Congress to protect us against catastrophe by meeting squarely our modern social and economic conditions.

We are at a crisis in our ability to proceed with that protection. It is a quiet crisis. There are no lines of depositors outside closed banks. But to the far-sighted it is far-reaching in its possibilities of injury to America.

I want to talk with you very simply tonight about the need for present action in this crisis – the need to meet the unanswered challenge of one-third of a Nation ill-nourished, ill-clad, ill-housed.

Last Thursday I described the American form of Government as a three-horse team provided by the Constitution to the American people so that their field might be plowed. The three horses are, of course, the Congress, the Executive and the Courts. Two of the horses, the Congress and the Executive, are pulling in unison today; the third is not. Those who have intimated that the President of the United States is trying to drive that team, overlook the simple fact that the President, as Chief Executive, is himself one of the three horses.

It is the American people themselves who are in the driver's seat. It is the American people themselves who want the furrow plowed.

It is the American people who expect the third horse to pull in unison with the other two.

I hope that you have re-read the Constitution of the United States in these past few weeks. Like the Bible, it ought to be read again and again.

It is an easy document to understand when you remember that it was called into being because the Articles of Confederation under which the original thirteen States tried to operate after the Revolution showed the need of a National Government with power enough to handle national problems. In its Preamble, the Constitution states that it was intended to form a more perfect Union and promote the general welfare; and the powers given to the Congress to carry out those purposes can best be described by saying that they were all the powers needed to meet each and every problem which then had a national character and which could not be met by merely local action.

But the framers went further. Having in mind that in succeeding generations many other problems then undreamed of would become national problems, they gave to the Congress the ample broad powers "to levy taxes . . . and provide for the common defense and general welfare of the United States."

That, my friends, is what I honestly believe to have been the clear and underlying purpose of the patriots who wrote a Federal Constituion to create a National Government with national power, intended as they said, "to form a more perfect union . . . for ourselves and our posterity."

For nearly twenty years there was no conflict between the Congress and the Court. Then, in 1803, Congress passed a statute which the Court said violated an express provision of the Constitution. The Court claimed the power to declare it unconstitutional and did so declare it. But a little later the Court itself admitted that it was an extraordinary power to exercise and through Mr. Justice Washington laid down this limitation upon it. He said: "It is but a decent respect due to the wisdom, the integrity and the patriotism of the Legislative body, by which any law is passed, to presume in favor of its validity until its violation of the Constitution is proved beyond all reasonable doubt."

But since the rise of the modern movement for social and economic progress through legislation, the Court has more and more often and more and more boldly asserted a power to veto laws passed by the Congress and by State Legislatures in complete disregard of this original limitation, which I have just read.

In the last four years the sound rule of giving statutes the benefit of all reasonable doubt has been cast aside. The Court has been acting not as a judicial body, but as a policy-making body.

When the Congress has sought to stabilize national agriculture, to improve the conditions of labor, to safeguard business against unfair competition, to protect our national resources, and in many other ways to serve our clearly national needs, the majority of the Court has been assuming the power to pass on the wisdom of these Acts of the Congress — and to approve or disapprove the public policy written into these laws.

That is not only my accusation. It is the accusation of most distinguished Justices of the present Supreme Court. I have not the time to quote to you all the language used by dissenting Justices in many of these cases. But in the case holding the Railroad Retirement Act unconstitutional, for instance, Chief Justice Hughes said in a dissenting opinion that the majority opinion was "a departure from sound principles," and placed "an unwarranted limitation upon the commerce clause." And three other Justices agreed with him.

In the case holding the Triple A unconstitutional, Justice Stone said of the majority opinion that it was a "tortured construction of the Constitution." And two other Justices agreed with him.

In the case holding the New York Minimum Wage Law unconstitutional, Justice Stone said that the majority were actually reading into the Constitution their own "personal economic predilections," and that if the legislative power is not left free to choose the methods of solving the problems of poverty, subsistence and health of large numbers in the community, then "government is to be rendered impotent." And two other Justices agreed with him.

In the face of these dissenting opinions, there is no basis for the claim made by some members of the Court that something in the Constitution has compelled them regretfully to thwart the will of the people.

In the face of such dissenting opinions, it is perfectly clear that, as Chief Justice Hughes has said: "We are under a Constitution but the Constitution is what the Judges say it is."

The Court, in addition to the proper use of its judicial functions, has improperly set itself up as a third house of the Congress—a super-legislature as one of the Justices has called it—reading into the Constitution words and implications which are not there, and which were never intended to be there.

We have, therefore, reached the point as a Nation where we must take action to save the Constitution from the Court and the Court from itself. We must find a way to take an appeal from the Supreme Court to the Constitution itself. We want a Supreme Court which will do justice under the Constitution — not over it. In our Courts we want a government of laws and not of men.

I want — as all Americans want — an independent judiciary as proposed by the framers of the Constitution. That means a Supreme Court that will enforce the Constitution as written—that will refuse to amend the Constitution by the arbitrary exercise of judicial power — amendment, in other words, by judicial say-so. It does not mean a judiciary so independent that it can deny the existence of facts which are universally recognized.

How then could we proceed to perform the mandate given us? It was said in last year's Democratic platform, and here are the words, "If these problems cannot be effectively solved within the Constitution, we shall seek such clarifying amendment as will assure the power to enact those laws, adequately to regulate commerce, protect public health and safety, and safeguard economic security." In other words, we said we would seek an amendment only if every other possible means by legislation were to fail.

When I commenced to review the situation with the problem squarely before me, I came by a process of elimination to the conclusion that short of amendments the only method which was clearly constitutional, and would would at the same time carry out other much needed reforms, was to infuse new blood into all our Courts. We must have men worthy and equipped to carry out impartial justice. But, at the same time, we must have Judges who will bring to the Courts a present-day sense of the Constitution – Judges who will retain in the Courts the judicial functions of a court, and reject the legislative powers which the Courts have today assumed.

It is well for us to remember that in forty-five out of the forty-eight States of the Union Judges are chosen not for life but for a period of years. In many states Judges must retire at the age of seventy. Congress has provided financial security by offering life pensions at full pay for Federal Judges on all Courts who are willing to retire at seventy. In the case of Supreme Court Justices that pension is $20,000. a year. But all Federal Judges, once appointed, can, if they choose, hold office for life, no matter how old they may get to be.

What is my proposal? It is simply this: Whenever a Judge or Justice of any Federal Court has reached the age of seventy and does not avail himself of the opportunity to retire on a pension, a new member shall be appointed by the President then in office, with the approval, as required by the Constituion, of the Senate of the United States.

That plan has two chief purposes. By bringing into the Judicial system a steady and continuing stream of new and younger blood, I hope, first, to make the administration of all Federal justice, from the bottom to the top, speedier and, therefore, less costly; secondly, to bring to the decision of social and economic problems younger men who have had personal experience and contact with modern facts and circumstances under which average men have to live and work. This plan will save our national Constitution from hardening of the judicial arteries.

The number of Judges to be appointed would depend wholly on the decision of present Judges now over seventy, or those who would subsequently reach the age of seventy.

If, for instance, any one of the six Justices of the Supreme Court now over the age of seventy should retire as provided under the plan, no additional place would be created. Consequently, although there never can be more than fifteen, there may be only fourteen, or thirteen, or twelve. And there may be only nine.

There is nothing novel or radical about this idea. It seeks to maintain the Federal bench in full vigor. It has been discussed and approved by many persons of high authority ever since a similar proposal passed the House of Representatives in 1869.

Why was the age fixed at seventy? Because the laws of many states, and the practice of the Civil Service, the regulations of the Army and Navy, and the rules of many of our universities and of almost every great private business enterprise, commonly fix the retirement age at seventy years or less.

The statute would apply to all the Courts in the Federal system. There is general approval so far as the lower Federal courts are concerned. The plan has met opposition only so far as the Supreme Court of the United States itself is concerned. But, my friends, if such a plan is good for the lower courts it certainly ought to be equally good for the highest Court from which there is no appeal.

Those opposing this plan have sought to arouse prejudice and fear by crying that I am seeking to "pack" the Supreme Court and that a baneful precedent will be established.

What do they mean by the words "packing the Supreme Court"?

Let me answer this question with a bluntness that will end all honest misunderstanding of my purposes.

If by that phrase "packing the Court" it is charged that I wish to place on the bench spineless puppets who would disregard the law and would decide specific cases as I wished them to be decided, I make this answer – that no President fit for his office would appoint, and no Senate of honorable men fit for their office would confirm, that kind of appointees to the Supreme Court.

But if by that phrase the charge is made that I would appoint and the Senate would confirm Justices worthy to sit beside present members of the Court who understand modern conditions – that I will appoint Justices who will not undertake to override the judgement of the Congress on legislative policy – that I will appoint Justices who will act as Justices and not as legislators – if the appointment of such Justices can be called "packing the Court," then I say that I, and with me the vast majority of the American people, favor doing just that thing – now.

Is it a dangerous precedent for the Congress to change the number of the Justices? The Congress has always had, and will have, that power. The number of Justices has been changed several times before—in the Administrations of John Adams and Thomas Jefferson—both of them signers of the Declaration of Independence – in the Administrations of Andrew Jackson, Abraham Lincoln and Ulysses S. Grant. . . .

Like all Americans, I regret the necessity of this controversy. But the welfare of the United States, and indeed of the Constitution itself, is what we all must think about first. Our difficulty with the Court today rises not from the Court as an institution but from human beings within it. But we cannot yield our constitutional destiny to the personal judgment of a few men who, being fearful of the future, would deny us the necessary means of dealing with the present.

This plan of mine is no attack on the Court; it seeks to restore the Court to its rightful and historic place in our system of Constitutional Government and to have it resume its high task of building anew on the Constitution "a system of living law." The Court itself can best undo what the Court has done. . . .

THE QUARANTINE SPEECH
October 5, 1937

*Speaking in Chicago on the occasion of a dedication of a
PWA bridge, the President abruptly seemed to challenge
the isolationists by calling for a "quarantine against aggressors." The speech met with opposition from isolationist leaders, although many Americans applauded it.
Roosevelt, though, pulled back from controversy by denying that he meant action.*

I am glad to come once again to Chicago and especially to have the
opportunity of taking part in the dedication of this important project of
civic betterment.

On my trip across the continent and back I have been shown many
evidences of the result of common-sense cooperation between municipalities and the Federal Government, and I have been greeted by tens
of thousands of Americans who have told me in every look and word
that their material and spiritual well-being has made great strides
forward in the past few years.

And yet, as I have seen with my own eyes the prosperous farms,
the thriving factories and the busy railroads — as I have seen the
happiness and security and peace which covers our wide land — almost
inevitably I have been compelled to contrast our peace with very different scenes being enacted in other parts of the world.

It is because the people of the United States under modern conditions must, for the sake of their own future, give thought to the rest
of the world, that I, as the responsible executive head of the nation, have
chosen this great inland city and this gala occasion to speak to you on
a subject of definite national importance.

The political situation in the world, which of late has been growing
progressively worse, is such as to cause grave concern and anxiety
to all the peoples and nations who wish to live in peace and amity with
their neighbors.

Some nine years ago the hopes of mankind for a continuing era of
international peace were raised to great heights when more than sixty
nations solemnly pledged themselves not to resort to arms in further-
ance of their national aims and politices. The high aspirations expressed in the Briand-Kellogg Peace Pact and the hopes for peace thus
raised have of late given way to a haunting fear of calamity.

The present reign of terror and international lawlessness began a
few years ago. It began through unjustified interference in the inter-

national affairs of other nations or the invasion of alien territory in violations of treaties, and has now reached a stage where they very foundations of civilization are seriously threatened.

The landmarks and traditions which have marked the progress of civilization toward a condition of law, order and justice are being wiped away.

Without a declaration of war and without warning or justification of any kind, civilians, including women and children, are being ruthlessly murdered with bombs from the air.

In times of so-called peace, ships are being attacked and sunk by submarines without cause or notice. Nations are fomenting and taking sides in civil warfare in nations that have never done them any harm. Nations claiming freedom for themselves deny it to others.

Innocent peoples and nations are being cruelly sacrificed to a greed for power and supremacy which is devoid of all sense of justice and humane consideration.

To paraphrase a recent author: "Perhaps we foresee a time when men, exultant in the technique of homicide, will rage so hotly over the world that every precious thing will be in danger, every book and picture and harmony, every treasure garnered through two millenniums, the small, the delicate, the defenseless – all will be lost or wrecked or utterly destroyed."

If those things come to pass in other parts of the world, let no one imagine that America will escape, that it may expect mercy, that this Western Hemisphere will not be attacked and that it will continue tranquilly and peacefully to carry on the ethics and the arts of civilization.

If those days come, "there will be no safety by arms, no help from authority, no answer in science. The storm will rage till every flower of culture is trampled and all human beings are leveled in a vast chaos."

If those days are not to come to pass – if we are to have a world in which we can breathe freely and live in amity without fear – the peace-loving nations must make a concerted effort to uphold laws and principles on which alone peace can rest secure.

The peace-loving nations must make a concerted effort in opposition to those violations of treaties and those ignorings of humane instincts which today are creating a state of international anarchy and instability from which there is no escape through mere isolation or neutrality.

Those who cherish their freedom and recognize and respect the equal right of their neighbors to be free and live in peace must work together for the triumph of law and moral principles in order that peace, justice and confidence may prevail in the world.

There must be a return to a belief in the pledged word, in the value of a signed treaty. There must be recognition of the fact that national morality is as vital as private morality.

A Bishop wrote me the other day:

"It seems to be that something greatly needs to be said in behalf of ordinary humanity against the present practice of carrying the horrors of war to helpless civilians, especially women and children.

"It may be that such a protest might be regarded by many, who claim to be realists, as futile, but may it not be that the heart of mankind is so filled with horror at the present needless suffering that that force could be mobilized in sufficient volume to lessen such cruelty in the days ahead?

"Even though it may take tweny years, which God forbid, for civilization to make effective its corporate protest against this barbarism, surely strong voices may hasten the day."

There is a solidarity and interdependence about the modern world, both technically and morally, which makes it impossible for any nation completely to isolate itself from economic and political upheavals in the rest of the world, especially when such upheavals appear to be spreading and not declining.

There can be no stability or peace either within nations or between nations except under laws and moral standards adhered to by all. International anarchy destroys every foundation for peace. It jeopardizes either the immediate or the future security of every nation, large or small.

It is, therefore, a matter of vital interest and concern to the people of the United States that the sanctity of international treaties and the maintenance of international morality be restored.

The overwhelming majority of the peoples and nations of the world today want to live in peace.

They seek the removal of barriers against trade.

They want to exert themselves in industry, in agriculture and in business that they may increase their wealth through the production of wealth-producing goods rather than striving to produce military planes and bombs and machine guns and cannon for the destruction of human lives and useful property.

In those nations of the world which seem to be piling armament on armament for purposes of aggression, and those other nations which fear acts of aggression against them and their security, a very high proportion of the national income is being spent directly for armaments. It runs from 30 to as high as 50 per cent.

The proportion that we in the United States spend is far less – 11 or 12 per cent.

How happy we are that the circumstances of the moment permit us to put our money into bridges and boulevards, dams and reforestation, the conservation of our soil and many other kinds of useful works, rather than into huge standing armies and vast supplies of implements of war.

I am compelled and you are compelled, nevertheless, to look ahead. The peace, the freedom and the security of 90 per cent of the population of the world is being jeopardized by the remaining 10 per cent who are threatening a breakdown of all international order and law.

Surely the 90 per cent who want to live in peace under law and in accordance with moral standards that have received almost universal acceptance through the centuries, can and must find some way to make their will prevail.

The situation is definitely of universal concern. The questions involved relate not merely to violations of specific provisions of particular treaties; they are questions of war and of peace, of international law, and especially of principles of humanity. It is true that they involve definite violations of agreements, and especially of the Covenant of the League of Nations, the Briand-Kellogg Pact and the Nine-Power Treaty. But they also involve problems of world economy, world security and world humanity.

It is true that the moral consciousness of the world must recognize the importance of removing injustices and well-founded grievances; but at the same time it must be aroused to the cardinal necessity of honoring sanctity of treaties, of respecting the rights and liberties of others and of putting an end to acts of international aggression.

It seems to be unfortunately true that the epidemic of world lawlessness is spreading.

When an epidemic of physical disease starts to spread, the community approves and joins in a quarantine of the patients in order to protect the health of the community against the spread of the disease.

It is my determination to pursue a policy of peace and to adopt every practicable measure to avoid involvement in war.

It ought to be inconceivable that in this modern era, and in the face of experience, any nation could be so foolish and ruthless as to run the risk of plunging the whole world into war by invading and violating, in contravention of solemn treaties, the territory of other nations that have done them no real harm and which are too weak to protect themselves adequately. Yet the peace of the world and the welfare and security of every nation is today being threatened by that very thing.

No nation which refuses to exercise forbearance and to respect the freedom and rights of others can long remain strong and retain the confidence and respect of other nations. No nation ever loses its dignity or good standing by conciliating its differences, and by exercising great patience with, and consideration for, the rights of other nations.

War is a contagion, whether it be declared or undeclared. It can engulf states and peoples remote from the original scene of hostilities. We are determined to keep out of war, yet we cannot insure ourselves against the disastrous effects of war and the dangers of involvement. We are adopting such measures as will minimize our risk of involvement, but we cannot have complete protection in a world of disorder in which confidence and security have broken down.

If civilization is to survive, the principles of the Prince of Peace must be restored. Shattered trust between nations must be revived.

Most important of all, the will for peace on the part of peace-loving nations must express itself to the end that nations that may be tempted to violate their agreements and the rights of others will desist from such a cause. There must be positive endeavors to preserve peace.

America hates war. America hopes for peace. Therefore America actively engages in the search for peace.

"DAGGER IN THE BACK" ADDRESS
June 10, 1940

*Speaking at the University of Virginia at Charlottesville
the President inserted into his speech, over the objec-
tions of Under Secretary of State Sumner Welles, who believed it undiplomatic, his famous reference to Mussolini's
attack on France after Hitler had brought that nation to her
knees. His speech challenged the isolationists by pledging the material resources of the United States to aid these
nations which are opposing the exponents of force, and re-
minding Americans that isolationists' concept of an
American "island" promised instead a "horrible nightmare" of a people in prison.*

President Newcomb, my friends of the University of Virginia.

I notice by the program that I am asked to address the classes of
1940. I avail myself of that privilege, but I also take this very happy
occasion to speak to many other classes —classes that have graduated
through all the years, classes that are still in the period of study,
classes not alone of the schools of learning of the nation, but classes
that have come up through the great schools of experience. In other
words, a cross-section, a cross-section just as you who graduate today
are a cross-section of the nation as a whole.

Every generation of young men and women in America has questions
to ask the world. Most of the time they are the simple but nevertheless
difficult questions — questions of work to do, opportunities to find, ambitions to satisfy.

But every now and again in the history of the republic a different
kind of question presents itself — a question that asks, not about the
future of an individual or even of a generation, but about the future of
the country, the future of the American people.

There was such a time at the beginning of our history, at the beginning of our history as a nation. Young people asked themselves in
those days what lay ahead, not for themselves, but for the new United
States.

There was such a time again in the seemingly endless years of the
war between the States. Young men and young women on both sides of
the line asked themselves, not what trades or professions they would
enter, what lives they would make, but what was to become of the country they had known.

There is such a time again today. Again today the young men and
the young women of America ask themselves with earnestness and with
deep concern this same question: "What is to become of the country
we know?"

Now they ask it with even greater anxiety than before. They ask, not only what the future holds for this republic, but what the future holds for all peoples and all nations that have been living under democratic forms of government — under the free institutions of a free people.

It is understandable to all of us, I think, that they shou d ask this question. They read the words of those who are telling them that the ideal of individual liberty, the ideal of free franchise, the ideal of peace through justice is a decadent ideal.

They read the word and hear the boast of those who say that a belief in force — force directed by self-chosen leaders — is the new and vigorous system which will overrun the earth. They have seen the ascendency of this philosophy of force in nation after nation where free institutions and individual liberties were once maintained.

It is natural and understandable that the younger generation should first ask itself what the extension of the philosophy of force to all the world would lead to ultimately. We see today, for example, in stark reality some of the consequences of what we call the machine age.

Where control of machines has been retained in the hands of mankind as a whole, untotaled benefits have accrued to mankind. For mankind was then the master: The machine was the servant.

But in this new system of force the mastery of the machine is not in the hands of mankind. It is in the control of infinitely small groups of individuals who rule without a single one of the democratic sanctions that we have known.

The machine in the hands of irresponsible conquerors becomes the master; mankind is not only the servant, it is the victim too. Such mastery abandons with deliberate contempt all of the moral values to which even this young country for more than 300 years has been accustomed and dedicated.

Surely the new philosophy proves from month to month that it could have no possible conception of the way of life or the way of thought of a nation whose origins go back to Jamestown and Plymouth Rock.

And conversely, neither those who spring from that ancient stock nor those who have come hither in later years can be indifferent to the destruction of freedom in their ancestral lands across the sea.

Perception of danger to our institutions may come slowly or it may come with a rush and shock as it has to the people of the United States in the past few months. This perception of danger — danger in a world-wide arena — has come to us clearly and over-whelmingly. We perceive the peril in this world-wide arena — an arena that may become so narrow that only the Americas will retain the ancient faiths.

Some indeed still hold to the now somewhat obvious delusion that we of the United States can safely permit the United States to become a lone island, a lone island in a world dominated by the philosophy of force.

Such an island may be the dream of those who still talk and vote as isolationists. Such an island represents to me and to the overwhelming majority of Americans today a helpless nightmare, the helpless nightmare of a people without freedom. Yes, the nightmare of a people lodged in prison, handcuffed, hungry and fed through the bars from day to day by the contemptuous, unpitying masters of other continents.

It is natural also that we should ask ourselves how now we can prevent the building of that prison and the placing of ourselves in the midst of it.

Let us not hesitate — all of us — to proclaim certain truths. Overwhelmingly we, as a nation, and this applies to all the other American nations, we are convinced that military and naval victory for the gods of force and hate would endanger the institutions of democracy in the Western World — and that equally, therefore, the whole of our sympathies lie with those nations that are giving their life blood in combat against those forces.

The people and Government of the United States have seen with the utmost regret and with grave disquiet the decision of the Italian Government to engage in the hostilities now raging in Europe.

More than three months ago the chief of the Italian Government sent me word that because of the determination of Italy to limit, so far as might be possible, the spread of the European conflict, more than two hundred millions of people in the region of the Mediterranean had been enabled to escape the suffering and the devastation of war.

I informed the chief of the Italian Government that this desire on the part of Italy to prevent the war from spreading met with full sympathy and response on the part of the government and the people of the United States, and I expressed the earnest hope of this government and of this people that this policy on the part of Italy might be continued. I made it clear that in the opinion of the Government of the United States any extension of hostilities in the region of the Mediterranean might result in the still greater enlargement of the scene of the conflict, the conflict in the Near East and in Africa, and that if this came to pass no one could foretell how much greater the theatre of war eventually might become.

Again, upon a subsequent occasion, not so far ago, recognizing that certain aspirations of Italy might form the basis of discussions between the powers most specifically concerned, I offered, in a message addressed to the chief of the Italian Government, to send to the Governments of France and Great Britain such specific indications of the desires of Italy to obtain readjustments with regard to her position as the chief of the Italian Government might desire to transmit through me.

While making it clear that the government of the United States in such an event could not and would not assume responsibility for the nature of the proposals submitted nor for agreements which might thereafter be reached, I proposed that if Italy would refrain from entering the war I would be willing to ask assurances from the other powers concerned that they would faithfully execute any agreement so reached, and that Italy's voice in any future peace conference would have the same authority as if Italy had actually taken part in the war as a belligerent.

Unfortunately, unfortunately to the regret of all of us, and to the regret of humanity, the chief of the Italian Government was unwilling to accept the procedure suggested, and he has made no counter-proposal. This government directed its efforts to doing what it could to work for the preservation of peace in the Mediterranean area, and it likewise expressed its willingness to endeavor to cooperate with the goverment of Italy when the appropriate occasion arose for the creation of a more stable world order, through the reduction of armaments and through the construction of a more liberal international economic system which would assure to all powers equality of opportunity in the world markets and in the securing of raw materials on equal terms.

I have likewise, of course, felt it necessary in my communications to Signor Mussolini to express the concern of the government of the United States because of the fact that any extension of the war in the region of the Mediterranean would inevitably result in great prejudice to the ways of life and government and to the trade and commerce of all the American republics.

The government of Italy has now chosen to preserve what it terms its "freedom of action" and to fulfill what it states are its promises to Germany. In so doing it has manifested disregard for the rights and security of other nations, disregard for the lives of the peoples of those nations which are directly threatened by the spread of this war; and has evinced its unwillingness to find the means through Pacific negotiations for the satisfaction of what it believes are its legitimate aspirations.

On this 10th day of June, 1940, the hand that held the dagger has struck it into the back of its neighbor.

On this 10th day of June, 1940, in this university founded by the first great American teacher of democracy, we send forth our prayers and our hopes to those beyond the seas who are maintining with magnificent valor their battle for freedom.

In our unity, in our American unity, we will pursue two obvious and simultaneous courses; we will extend to the opponents of force the material resources of this nation and, at the same time, we will harness and speed up the use of those resources in order that we ourselves in the Americas may have equipment and training equal to the task of any emergency and every defense.

All roads leading to the accomplishment of these objectives must be kept clear of obstructions. We will not slow down or detour. Signs and signals call for speed – full speed ahead.

Yes, it is right that each new generation should ask questions. But in recent months the principal question has been somewhat simplified. Once more the future of the nation and the future of the American people is at stake.

We need not and we will not, in any way, abandon our continuing efforts to make democracy work within our borders. Yes, we still insist on the need for vast improvements in our own social and economic life.

But that, that is a component part of national defense itself.

The program unfolds swiftly and into that program will fit the responsibility and the opportunity of every man and woman in the land to preserve our heritage in days of peril.

I call for effort, courage, sacrifice, devotion. Granting the love of freedom, all of these are possible.

And the love of freedom is still fierce, still steady in the nation today.

ANNUAL MESSAGE TO CONGRESS
January 6, 1941

President Roosevelt called for a world based on his earlier "Four Freedoms," and gave it a sharper meaning by listing a specific economic bill of rights.

Mr. Speaker, members of the 77th Congress:

I address you, the members of this new Congress, at a moment unprecedented in the history of the union. I use the word "unprecedented" because at no previous time has American security been as seriously threatened from without as it is today.

Since the permanent formation of our government under the Constitution in 1789, most of the periods of crisis in our history have related to our domestic affairs. And, fortunately, only one of these – the four-year war between the States – ever threatened our national unity. Today, thank God, 130,000,000 Americans in forty-eight States have forgotten points of the compass in our national unity.

It is true that prior to 1914 the United States often has been disturbed by events in other continents. We have been engaged in two wars with European nations and in a number of undeclared wars in the West Indies, in the Mediterranean and in the Pacific, for the maintenance of American rights and for the principles of peaceful commerce. But in no case had a serious threat been raised against our national safety or our continued independence.

What I seek to convey is the historic truth that the United States as a nation has at all times maintained opposition – clear, definite opposition – to any attempt to lock us in behind an ancient Chinese wall while the procession of civilization went past. Today, thinking of our children and of their children, we oppose enforced isolation for ourselves or for any other part of the Americas.

That determination of ours, extending over all these years, was proved, for example, in the early days during the quarter century of wars following the French Revolution.

While the Napoleonic struggle did threaten interests of the United States because of the French foothold in the West Indies and in Louisiana, and while we engaged in the War of 1812 to vindicate our right to peaceful trade, it is nevertheless clear that neither France nor Great Britain nor any other nation was aiming at domination of the whole world.

And in like fashion, from 1815 to 1914 – ninety-nine years – no single war in Europe or in Asia constituted a real threat against our future or against the future of any other American nation.

Except in the Maximilian interlude in Mexico, no foreign power sought to establish itself in this hemisphere. And the strength of the British fleet in the Atlantic has been a freindly strength; it is still a friendly strength.

Even when the World War broke out in 1914 it seemed to contain only a small threat of danger to our own American future. But as time went on, as we remember, the American people began to visualize what the downfall of democratic nations might mean to our own democracy.

We need not overemphasize imperfections in the peace of Versailles. We need not harp on failure of the democracies to deal with problems of world reconstruction. We should remember that the peace of 1919 was far less unjust than the kind of pacification whcih began even before Munich, and which is being carried on under the new order of tyranny that seeks to spread over every continent today.

The American people have unalterably set their faces against that tyranny.

I suppose that every realist knows that the democratic way of life is at this moment being directly assailed in every part of the world – assailed either by arms or by secret spreading of poisonous propaganda by those who seek to destroy unity and promote discords in nations that are still at peace.

During sixteen long months this assault has blotted out the whole pattern of democratic life in an appaling number of independent nations, great and small. And the assailants are still on the march, threatening other nations, great and small.

Therefore, as your President, performing my constitutional duty to "give to the Congress information of the state of the union," I find it unhappily necessary to report that the future and the safety of our country and of our democracy are overwhelmingly involved in events far beyond our borders.

Armed defense of democratic existence is now being gallantly waged in four continents. If that defense fails, all the population and all the resources of Europe and Asia, Africa and Australia will be dominated by conquerors. And let us remember that the total of those populations in those four continents, the total of those populations and their resources greatly exceeds the sum total of the population and the resources of the whole of the Western Hemisphere – yes, many times over.

In times like these it is immature – and, incidentally, untrue – for anybody to brag that an unprepared America, single-handed and with one hand tied behind its back, can hold off the whole world.

No realistic American can expect from a dictator's peace international generosity, or return to true independence, or world disarmament, or freedom of expression, or freedom of religion — or even good business. Such a peace would bring no security for us or for our neighbors. Those who would give up essential liberty to purchase a little temporary safety deserve neither liberty nor safety.

As a nation we may take pride in the fact that we are soft-hearted; but we cannot afford to be soft-headed. We must always be wary of those who with sounding brass and a tinkling cymbal preach the ism of appeasement. We must especially beware of that small group of selfish men who would clip the wings of the American eagle to feather their own nests.

I have recently pointed out how quickly the tempo of modern warfare could bring into our very midst the physical attack which we must eventually expect if the dictator nations win this war.

There is much loose talk of our immunity from immediate and direct invasion from across the seas. Obviously, as long as the British Navy retains its power, no such danger exists. Even if there were no British Navy it is not probable that any enemy would be stupid enough to attack us by landing troops in the United States from across thousands of miles of ocean, until it had acquired strategic bases from which to operate.

But we learn much from the lessons of the past years in Europe — particularly the lesson of Norway, whose essential seaports were captured by treachery and surprise built up over a series of years.

The first phase of the invasion of this hemisphere would not be the landing of regular troops. The necessary strategic points would be occupied by secret agents and by their dupes — and great numbers of them are already here and in Latin America.

As long as the aggressor nations maintain the offensive they, not we, will choose the time and the place, and the method of their attack.

And that is why the future of all the American Republics is today in serious danger. That is why this annual message to the Congress is unique in our history. That is why every member of the executive branch of the government and every member of the Congress face great responsibiltiy — great accountability.

The need of the moment is that our actions and our policy should be devoted primarily — almost exclusively — to meeting this foreign peril. For all our domestic problems are now a part of the great emergency.

Just as our national policy in internal affairs has been based upon a decent respect for the rights and the dignity of all of our fellow men within our gates, so our national policy in foreign affairs has been based on a decent respect for the rights and the dignity of all nations, large and small. And the justice of morality must and will win in the end.

Our national policy is this:

First, by an impressive expression of the public will and without regard to partisanship, we are committed to all-inclusive national defense.

Second, by an impressive expression of the public will and without regard to partisanship, we are committed to full support of all those resolute people everywhere who are resisting aggression and are thereby keeping war away from our hemisphere. By this support we express our determination that the democratic cause shall prevail, and we strengthen the defense and the security of our own nation.

Third, by an impressive expression of the public will and without regard to partisanship, we are committed to the proposition that principles of morality and considerations for our own security will never permit us to acquiesce in a peace dictated by aggressors and sponsored by appeasers. We know that enduring peace cannot be bought at the cost of other people's freedom.

In the recent national election there was no substantial difference between the two great parties in respect to that national policy. No issue was fought out on this line before the American electorate. And today it is abundantly evident that American citizens everywhere are demanding and supporting speedy and complete action in recognition of obvious danger.

Therefore, the immediate need is a swift and driving increase in our armament production. Leaders of industry and labor have responded to our summons. Goals of speed have been set. In some cases these goals are being reached ahead of time. In some cases we are on schedule; in other cases there are slight but not serious delays. And in some cases – and, I am sorry to say, very important cases – we are still concerned by the slowness of the accomplishment of our plans.

The Army and Navy, however, have made substantial progress during the past year. Actual experience is improving and speeding up our methods of production with every passing day. And today's best is not good enough for tomorrow.

I am not satisfied with the progress thus far made. The men in charge of the program represent the best in training, in ability and in patriotism. They are not satisfied with the progress thus far made. None of us will be satisfied until the job is done.

No matter whether the original goal was set too high or too low, our objective is quicker and better results.

To give you two illustrations:

We are behind schedule in turning out finished airplanes. We are working day and night to solve the innumerable problems and to catch up.

We are ahead of schedule in building warships, but we are working to get even further ahead of that schedule.

To change a whole nation from a basis of peacetime production of implements of peace to a basis of wartime production of implements of war is no small task. The greatest difficulty comes at the beginning of the program, when new tools, new plant facilities, new assembly lines, new shipways must first be constructed before the actual material begins to flow steadily and speedily from them.

The Congress, of course, must rightly keep itself informed at all times of the progress of the program. However, there is certain information, as the Congress itself will readily recognize, which, in the interests of our own security and those of the nations that we are supporting, must of needs be kept in confidence.

New circumstances are constantly begetting new needs for our safety. I shall ask this Congress for greatly increased new appropriations and authorizations to carry on what we have begun.

I also ask this Congress for authority and for funds sufficient to manufacture additional munitions and war supplies of many kinds, to be turned over to those nations which are now in actual war with aggressor nations. Our most useful and immediate role is to act as an arsenal for them as well as for ourselves. They do not need manpower, but they do need billions of dollars' worth of the weapons of defense.

The time is near when they will not be able to pay for them all in ready cash. We cannot, and we will not, tell them that they must surrender merely because of present inability to pay for the weapons which we know they must have.

I do not recommend that we make them a loan of dollars with which to pay for these weapons — a loan to be repaid in dollars. I recommend that we make it possible for those nations to continue to obtain war materials in the United States, fitting their orders into our own program. And nearly all of their material would, if the time ever came, be useful in our own defense.

For what we send abroad we shall be repaid, repaid with a reasonable time following the close of hostilities, repaid in similar materials, or at our option in other goods of many kinds which they can produce and which we need.

Let us say to the democracies:

We Americans are vitally concerned in your defense of freedom. We are putting forth our energies, our resources and our organizing powers to give you the strength to regain and maintain a free world. We shall send you in ever-increasing numbers, ships, planes, tanks, guns. That is our purpose and our pledge.

In fulfillment of this purpose we will not be intimidated by the threats of dictators that they will regard as a breach of international law or as an act of war our aid to the democracies which dare to resist their aggression. Such aid is not an act of war, even if a dictator should unilaterally proclaim it so to be.

And when the dictators — if the dictators — are ready to make war upon us, they will not wait for an act of war on our part.

They did not wait for Norway or Belgium or the Netherlands to commit an act of war. Their only interest is in a new one-way international law which lacks mutuality in its observances and therefore becomes an instrument of oppression. The happiness of future generations of Americans may well depend on how effective and how immediate we can make our aid felt. No one can tell the exact character of the emergency situations that we may be called upon to meet. The nation's hands must not be tied when the nation's life is in danger.

Yes, and we must prepare, all of us prepare, to make the sacrifices that the emergency — almost as serious as war itself —demands. Whatever stands in the way of speed and efficiency in defense, in defense preparations at any time, must give way to the national need.

A free nation has the right to expect full cooperation from all groups. A free nation has the right to look to the leaders of business, of labor and of agriculture to take the lead in stimulating effort, not among other groups but within their own groups.

The best way of dealing with the few slackers or troublemakers in our midst is, first, to shame them by patriotic example, and if that fails, to use the sovereignty of government to save government.

As men do not live by bread alone, they do not fight by armament alone. Those who man our defenses and those behind them who build our defenses must have the stamina and the courage which come from unshakable belief in the manner of life which they are defending. The mighty action that we are calling for cannot be based on a disregard for all the things worth fighting for.

The nation takes great satisfaction and much strength from the things which have been done to make its people conscious of their individual stakes in the preservation of democratic life in America. Those things have toughened the fiber of our people, have renewed their faith and strengthened their devotion to the institutions we make ready to protect.

Certainly this is no time for any of us to stop thinking about the social and economic problems which are the root cause of the social revolution which is today a supreme factor in the world. For there is nothing mysterious about the foundations of a healthy and strong democracy.

The basic things expected by our people of their political and economic systems are simple. They are:

Equality of opportunity for youth and for others.
Jobs for those who can work.
Security for those who need it.
The ending of special privilege for the few.
The preservation of civil liberties for all.
The employment of the fruits of scientific progress in a wider and constantly rising standard of living.

These are the simple, the basic things that must never be lost sight of in the turmoil and unbelievable complexity of our modern world. The inner and abiding strength of our economic and political systems is dependent upon the degree to which they fulfill these expectations.

Many subjects connected with our social economy call for immediate improvement. As examples:

We should bring more citizens under the coverage of old-age pension and unemployment insurance.

We should widen the opportunities for adequate medical care.

We should plan a better system by which persons deserving or needing gainful employment may obtain it.

I have called for personal sacrifice, and I am assured of the willingness of almost all Americans to respond to that call. A part of the sacrifice means the payment of more money in taxes. In my budget message I will recommend that a greater portion of this great defense program be paid for from taxation than we are paying for today. No person should try, or be allowed to get rich out of the program, and the principle of tax payments in accordance with ability to pay should be constantly before our eyes to guide our legislation.

If the Congress maintains these principles the voters, putting patriotism ahead of pocketbooks, will give you their applause.

In the future days which we seek to make secure, we look forward to a world founded upon four essential human freedoms.

The first is freedom of speech and expression — everywhere in the world.

The second is freedom of every person to worship God in his own way — everywhere in the world.

The third is freedom from want, which, translated into world terms, means economic understanding which will secure to every nation a healthy peacetime life for its inhabitants – everywhere in the world.

The fourth is freedom from fear, which, translated into world terms means a world-wide reduction of armaments to such a point and in such a thorough fashion that no nation will be in a position to commit an act of physical aggression against any neighbor – anywhere in the world.

That is no vision of a distant millenium. It is a definite basis for a kind, of world attainable in our own time and generation. That kind of world is the very antithesis of the so-called "new order" of tyranny which the dictators seek to create with the crash of a bomb.

To that new order we oppose the greater conception – the moral order. A good society is able to face schemes of world domination and foreign revolutions alike without fear.

Since the beginning of our American history we have been engaged in change, in a perpetual, peaceful revolution, a revolution which goes on steadily, quietly, adjusting itself to changing conditions without the concentration camp or the quicklime in the ditch. The world order which we seek is the cooperation of free countries, working together in a friendly, civilized society.

This nation has placed its destiny in the hands, heads and hearts of its millions of free men and women, and its faith in freedom under the guidance of God. Freedom means the supremacy of human rights everywhere. Our support goes to those who struggle to gain those rights and keep them. Our strength is our unity of purpose.

To that high concept there can be no end save victory.

THIRD INAUGURAL ADDRESS
January 20, 1941

As the President began an unprecedented third term, he turned to a tone of abstract philosophizing about democracy. The speech, prepared with help from his poet friend, Archibald MacLeish, fell flat.

On each national day of inauguration since 1789, the people have renewed their sense of dedication to the United States.

In Washington's day the task of the people was to create and weld together a nation.

In Lincoln's day the task of the people was to preserve that Nation from disruption from within.

In this day the task of the people is to save that Nation and its institutions from disruption from without.

To us there has come a time, in the midst of swift happenings, to pause for a moment and take stock—to recall what our place in history has been, and to rediscover what we are and what we may be. If we do not, we risk the real peril of inaction.

Lives of nations are determined not by the count of years, but by the lifetime of the human spirit. The life of a man is three-score years and ten: A little more, a little less. The life of a nation is the fullness of the measure of its will to live.

There are men who doubt this. There are men who believe that democracy, as a form of Government and a frame of life, is limited or measured by a kind of mystical and artificial fate — that, for some unexplained reason, tyranny and slavery have become the surging wave of the future — and that freedom is an ebbing tide.

But we Americans know that this is not true.

Eight years ago, when the life of this Republic seemed frozen by a fatalistic terror, we proved that this is not true. We were in the midst of shock — but we acted. We acted quickly, boldly, decisively.

These later years have been living years — fruitful years for the people of this democracy. For they have brought to us greater security and, I hope, a better understanding that life's ideals are to be measured in other than material things.

Most vital to our present and our future is this experience of a democracy which successfully survived crisis at home; put away many evil things; built new structures on enduring lines; and, through it all, maintained the fact of its democracy.

For action has been taken within the three-way framework of the Constitution of the United States. The coordinate branches of the Government continue freely to function. The Bill of Rights remains inviolate. The freedom of elections is wholly maintained. Prophets of the downfall of American democracy have seen their dire predictions come to nought.

Democracy is not dying.

We know it because we have seen it revive — and grow.

We know it cannot die — because it is built on the unhampered initiative of individual men and women joined together in a common enterpriese — an enterprise undertaken and carried through by the free expression of a free majority.

We know it because democracy alone, of all forms of government, enlists the full force of men's enlightened will.

We know it because democracy alone has constructed an unlimited civilization capable of infinite progress in the improvement of human life.

We know it because, if we look below the surface, we sense it still spreading on every continent — for it is the most humane, the most advanced, and in the end the most unconquerable of all forms of human society.

A nation, like a person, has a body — a body that must be fed and clothed and housed, invigorated and rested, in a manner that measures up to the objectives of our time.

A nation, like a person, has a mind — a mind that must be kept informed and alert, that must know itself, that understands the hopes and the needs of its neighbors — all the other nations that live within the narrowing circle of the world.

And a nation, like a person, has something deeper, something more permanent, something larger than the sum of all its parts. It is that something which matters most to its future — which calls forth the most sacred guarding of its present.

It is a thing for which we find it difficult — even impossible — to hit upon a single, simple word.

And yet we all understand what it is — the spirit — the faith of America. It is the product of centuries. It was born in the multitudes of those who came from many lands — some of high degree, but mostly plain people, who sought here, early and late, to find freedom more freely.

The democratic aspiration is no mere recent phase in human history. It is human history. It permeated the ancient life of early peoples. It blazed anew in the middle ages. It was written in Magna Carta.

In the Americas its impact has been irresistible. America has been the New World in all tongues, to all peoples, not because this continent was a new-found land, but because all those who came here believed they could create upon this continent a new life – a life that should be new in freedom.

Its vitality was written into our own Mayflower Compact, into the Declaration of Independence, into the Constitution of the United States, into the Gettysburg Address.

Those who first came here to carry out the longings of their spirit, and the millions who followed, and the stock that sprang from them– all have moved forward constantly and consistently toward an ideal which in itself has gained stature and clarity with each generation.

The hopes of the Republic cannot forever tolerate either undeserved poverty or self-serving wealth.

We know that we still have far to go; that we must more greatly build the security and the opportunity and the knowledge of every citizen, in the measure justified by the resources and the capacity of the land.

But it is not enough to achieve these purposes alone. It is not enough to clothe and feed the body of this Nation, and instruct and inform its mind. For there is also the spirit. And of the three, the greatest is the spirit.

Without the body and the mind, as all men know, the Nation could not live.

But if the spirit of America were killed, even though the Nation's body and mind, constricted in an alien world, lived on, the America we know would have perished.

That spirit – that faith – speaks to us in our daily lives in ways often unnoticed, because they seem so obvious. It speaks to us here in the Capital of the Nation. It speaks to us through the processes of governing in the sovereignties of 48 States. It speaks to us in our counties, in our cities, in our towns, and in our villages. It speaks to us from the other nations of the hemisphere, and from those across the seas – the enslaved, as well as the free. Sometimes we fail to hear or heed these voices of freedom because to us the privilege of our freedom is such an old, old story.

The destiny of America was proclaimed in words of prophecy spoken by our first President in his first inaugural in 1789 – words almost directed, it would seem, to this year of 1941: "The preservation of the sacred fire of liberty and the destiny of the republican model of government are justly considered * * * deeply, * * * finally, staked on the experiment intrusted to the hands of the American people."

If we lose that sacred fire — if we let it be smothered with doubt and fear — then we shall reject the destiny which Washington strove so valiantly and so triumphantly to establish. The preservation of the spirit and faith of the Nation does, and will, furnish the highest justification for every sacrifice that we may make in the cause of national defense.

In the face of great perils never before encountered, our strong purpose is to protect and to perpetuate the integrity of democracy.

For this we muster the spirit of America, and the faith of America.

We do not retreat. We are not content to stand still. As Americans, we go forward, in the service of our country, by the will of God.

WAR MESSAGE TO CONGRESS
December 8, 1941

The day after Pearl Harbor, and thirty-three minutes after
minutes after this speech, Congress, by a unanimous voie
of the Senate and by a vote of 388—1 in the House, de-
clared that a state of war existed by act of Japan.

Yesterday, December 7, 1941 — a date which will live in infamy — the United States of America was suddenly and deliberately attacked by naval and air forces of the Empire of Japan.

The United States was at peace with that nation and, at the solicitation of Japan, was still in conversation with its Government and its Emperor looking toward the maintenance of peace in the Pacific. Indeed, one hour after Japanese air squadrons had commenced bombing in the American Island of Oahu, the Japanese Ambassador to the United States and his colleague delivered to our Secretary of State a formal reply to a recent American message. And while this reply stated that it seemed useless to continue the existing diplomatic negotiations, it contained no threat or hint of war or of armed attack.

It will be recorded that the distance of Hawaii from Japan makes it obvious that the attack was deliberately planned many days or even weeks ago. During the intervening time the Japanese Government has deliberately sought to deceive the United States by false statements and expressions of hope for continued peace.

The attack yesterday on the Hawaiian Islands has caused severe damage to American naval and military forces. I regret to tell you that very many American lives have been lost. In addition American ships have been reported torpedoed on the high seas between San Francisco and Honolulu.

Yesterday the Japanese Government also launched an attack against Malaya.

Last night Japanese forces attacked Hong Kong.

Last night Japanese forces attacked Guam.

Last night Japanese forces attacked the Philippine Islands.

Last night the Japanese attacked Wake Island.

And this morning the Japanese attacked Midway Island.

Japan has, therefore, undertaken a surprise offensive extending throughout the Pacific area. The facts of yesterday and today speak for themselves. The people of the United States have already formed their opinions and well understand the implications to the very life and safety of our nation.

As Commander-in-Chief of the Army and Navy I have directed that all measures be taken for our defense.

But always will our whole nation remember the character of the onslaught against us.

No matter how long it may take us to overcome this premeditated invasion, the American people in their righteous might will win through to absolute victory.

I believe that I interpret the will of the Congress and of the people when I assert that we will not only defend ourselves to the uttermost but will make it very certain that this form of treachery shall never again endanger us.

Hostilities exist. There is no blinking at the fact that our people, our territory and our interests are in grave danger.

With confidence in our armed forces — with the unbounding determination of our people — we will gain the inevitable triumph — so help us God.

I ask that the Congress declare that since the unprovoked and dastardly attack by Japan on Sunday, December seventh, 1941, a state of war has existed between the United States and the Japanese Empire.

FIRESIDE CHAT ON PEARL HARBOR
December 9, 1941

*The President went on radio to give the American people
an early estimate of the losses at Pearl Harbor after item-
izing a decade of aggression by Japan and her Axis part-
ners, Germany and Italy. After Germany and Italy had formally declared war two days later, Congress unanimously
voted to accept Roosevelt's message on December 11 asking that a state of war existed between the United States
and those two nations.*

My fellow-Americans:

The sudden criminal attacks perpetrated by the Japanese in the
Pacific provide the climax of a decade of international immorality.

Powerful and resourceful gangsters have banded together to make
war upon the whole human race. Their challenge has now been flung
at the United States of America. The Japanese have treacherously
violated the long-standing peace between us. Many American soldiers
and sailors have been killed by enemy action. American ships have
been sunk; American airplanes have been destroyed.

The Congress and the people of the United States have accepted that
challenge.

Together with other free peoples, we are now fighting to maintain
our right to live among our world neighbors in freedom and in common
decency, without fear of assault.

I have prepared the full record of our past relations with Japan, and
it will be submitted to the Congress. It begins with the visit of Com-
modore Perry to Japan eighty-eight years ago. It ends with the visit
of two Japanese emissaries to the Secretary of State last Sunday, an
hour after Japanese forces had loosed their bombs and machine guns
against our flag, our forces and our citizens.

I can say with utmost confidence that no Americans today or a
thousand years hence need feel anything but pride in our patience and in
our efforts through all the years toward achieving a peace in the Pacific which would be fair and honorable to every nation, large or small.
And no honest person, today or a thousand years hence, will be able to
suppress a sense of indignation and horror at the treachery committed
by the military dictators of Japan under the very shadow of the flag
of peace borne by their special envoys in our midst.

The course that Japan has followed for the past ten years in Asia
has paralleled the course of Hitler and Mussolini in Europe and in

Africa. Today, it has become far more than a parallel. It is collaboration, actual collaboration, so well calculated that all the continents of the world, and all the oceans, are now considered by the Axis strategists as one gigantic battlefield.

In 1931, ten years ago, Japan invaded Manchukuo – without warning.

In 1935, Italy invaded Ethiopia – without warning.

In 1938, Hitler occupied Austria – without warning.

In 1939, Hitler invaded Czechoslovakia – without warning.

Later in 1939 Hitler invaded Poland – without warning.

In 1940, Hitler invaded Norway, Denmark, the Netherlands, Belgium and Luxemburg – without warning.

In 1940, Italy attacked France and later Greece – without warning.

And in this year, 1941, the Axis Powers attacked Yugoslavia and Greece and they dominated the Balkans – without warning.

In 1941 also, Hitler invaded Russia – without warning.

And now Japan has attacked Malaya and Thailand – and the United States – without warning.

It is all of one pattern.

We are now in this war. We are all in it – all the way. Every single man, woman and child is a partner in the most tremendous undertaking of our American history. We must share together the bad news and the good news, the defeats and the victories – the changing fortunes of war.

So far, the news has been all bad. We have suffered a serious setback in Hawaii. Our forces in the Philippines, which include the brave people of that commonwealth, are taking punishment, but are defending themselves vigorously. The reports from Guam and Wake and Midway Islands are still confused, but we must be prepared for the announcement that all these three outposts have been seized.

The casualty lists of these first few days will undoubtedly be large. I deeply feel the anxiety of all of the families of the men in our armed forces and the relatives of people in cities which have been bombed. I can only give them my solemn promise that they will get news just as quickly as possible.

This government will put its trust in the stamina of the American people and will give the facts to the public just as soon as two conditions have been fulfilled: first, that the information has been definitely and officially confirmed, and, second, that the release of the information at the time it is received will not prove valuable to the enemy directly or indirectly.

Most ernestly I urge my countrymen to reject all rumors. These ugly little hints of complete disaster fly thick and fast in wartime. They have to be examined and appraised.

As an example, I can tell you frankly that until further surveys are made, I have not sufficient information to state the exact damage which has been done to our naval vessels at Pearl Harbor. Admittedly the damage is serious. But no one can say how serious until we know how much of this damage can be repaired and how quickly the necessary repairs can be made.

I cite as another example a statement made on Sunday night that a Japanese carrier had been located and sunk off the Canal Zone. And when you hear statements that are attributed to what they call "an authoritative source," you can be reasonably sure from now on that under these war circumstances the "authoritative source" is not any person in authority.

Many rumors and reports which we now hear originate, of course, with enemy sources. For instance, today the Japanese are claiming that as a result of their one action against Hawaii they have gained naval supremacy in the Pacific. This is an old trick of propaganda which has been used innumerable times by the Nazis. The purposes of such fantastic claims are, of course, to spread fear and confusion among us and to goad us into revealing military information which our enemies are desperately anxious to obtain.

Our government will not be caught in this obvious trap — and neither will the people of the United States.

It must be remembered by each and every one of us that our free and rapid communication these days must be greatly restricted in wartime. It is not possible to receive full, speedy, accurate reports from distant areas of combat. This is particularly true where naval operations are concerned. For in these days of the marvels of radio it is often impossible for the commanders of various units to report their activities by radio, for the very simple reason that this informa- tion would become available to the enemy, and would disclose their position and their plan of defense or attack.

Of necessity there will be delays in officially confirming or deny- ing reports of operations, but we will not hide facts from the country if we know the facts and if the enemy will not be aided by their dis- closure.

To all newspapers and radio stations — all those who reach the eyes and ears of the American people — I say this: You have a most grave responsibility to the nation now and for the duration of this war.

If you feel that your government is not disclosing enough of the truth, you have every right to say so. But — in the absence of all the facts, as revealed by official sources — you have no right in the ethics of patriotism to deal out unconfirmed reports in such a way as to make people believe that they are gospel truth.

Every citizen, in every walk of life, shares this same responsibility. The lives of our soldiers and sailors — the whole future of this nation — depend upon the manner in which each and every one of us fulfills his obligation to our country.

Now a word about the recent past — and the future. A year and a half has elapsed since the fall of France, when the whole world first realized the mechanized might which the Axis nations had been building for so many years. America has used that year and a half to great advantage. Knowing that the attack might reach us in all too short a time, we immediately began greatly to increase our industrial strength and our capacity to meet the demands of modern warfare.

Precious months were gained by sending vast quantities of our war material to the nations of the world still able to resist Axis aggression. Our policy rested on the fundamental truth that the defense of any country resisting Hitler or Japan was in the long run the defense of our own country. That policy has been justified. It has given us time, invaluable time, to build our American assembly lines of production.

Assembly lines are now in operation. Others are being rushed to completion. A steady stream of tanks and planes. of guns, ships, and shells and equipment—that is what these eighteen months have given us.

But it is all only a beginning of what still has to be done. We must be set to face a long war against crafty and powerful bandits. The attack at Pearl Harbor can be repeated at any one of many points on both oceans and along both our coast lines and against all the rest of the hemisphere.

It will not only be a long war, it will be a hard war. That is the basis on which we now lay all our plans. That is the yardstick by which we measure what we shall need and demand — money, materials, doubled and quadrupled production — ever increasing. The production must be not only for our own Army and Navy and air forces. It must reinforce the other armies and navies and air forces fighting the Nazis and the war lords of Japan throughout the Americas and throughout the world.

I have been working today on the subject of production. Your government has decided on two broad policies.

The first is to speed up all existing production by working on a seven-day-week basis in every war industry, including the production of essential raw materials.

The second policy, now being put into form, is to rush additions to the capacity of production by building more new plants, by adding to old plants, and by using the many smaller plants for war needs.

Over the hard road of the past months we have at times met obstacles and difficulties, divisions and disputes, indifference and callousness. That is now all past — and, I am sure, forgotten.

The fact is that the country now has an organization in Washington built around men and women who are recognized experts in their own fields. I think the country knows that the people who are actually responsible in each and every one of these many fields are pulling together with a teamwork that has never before been excelled.

On the road ahead there lies hard work — gruelling work — day and night, every hour and every minute.

I was about to add that ahead there lies sacrifice for all of us.

But it is not correct to use that word. The United States does not consider it a sacrifice to do all one can, to give one's best to our nation, when the nation is fighting for its existence and its future life.

It is not a sacrifice for any man, old or young, to be in the Army or the Navy of the United States. Rather is it a privilege.

It is not a sacrifice for the industrialist or the wage-earner, the farmer or the shopkeeper, the trainman or the doctor, to pay more taxes, to buy more bonds, to forego extra profits, to work longer or harder at the task for which he is best fitted. Rather, it is a privilege.

It is not a sacrifice to do without many things to which we are accustomed if the national defense calls for doing without them.

A review this morning leads me to the conclusion that at present we shall not have to curtail the normal use of articles of food. There is enough food today for all of us and enough left over to send to those who are fighting on the same side with us.

But there will be a clear and definite shortage of metals for many kinds of civilian use for the very good reason that in our increased program we shall need for war purposes more than half of that portion of the principal metals which during the past year have gone into articles for civilian use. Yes, we shall have to give up many things entirely.

And I am sure that the people in every part of the nation are prepared in their individual living to win this war. I am sure that they will cheerfully help to pay a large part of its financial cost while it goes on. I am sure they will cheerfully give up those material things that they are asked to give up.

And I am sure that they will retain all those great spiritual things without which we cannot win through.

I repeat that the United States can accept no result save victory, final and complete. Not only must the shame of Japanese treachery be wiped out, but the sources of international brutality, wherever they exist, must be absolutely and finally broken.

In my message to the Congress yesterday I said that we "will make very certain that this form of treachery shall never endanger us again." In order to achieve that certainty, we must begin the great task that is before us by abandoning once and for all the illusion that we can ever again isolate ourselves from the rest of humanity.

In these past few years — and, most violently, in the past few days— we have learned a terrible lesson.

It is our obligation to our dead—it is our sacred obligation to their children and to our children — that we must never forget what we have learned.

And what we have learned is this:

There is no such thing as security for any nation — or any individual — in a world ruled by the principles of gangsterism.

There is no such thing as impregnable defense against powerful aggressors who sneak up in the dark and strike without warning.

We have learned that our ocean-girt hemisphere is not immune from severe attack — that we cannot measure our safety in terms of miles on any map any more.

We may acknowledge that our enemies have performed a brilliant feat of deception, perfectly timed and executed with great skill. It was a thoroughly dishonorable deed, but we must face the fact that modern warfare as conducted in the Nazi manner is a dirty business. We don't like it — we didn't want to get in it — but we are in it and we're going to fight it with everything we've got.

I do not think any American has any doubt of our ability to administer proper punishment to the perpetrators of these crimes.

Your government knows that for weeks Germany has been telling Japan that if Japan did not attack the United States, Japan would not share in dividing the spoils with Germany when peace came. She was promised by Germany that if she came in she would receive the complete and perpetual control of the whole of the Pacific area — and that means not only the Far East, but also all of the islands in the Pacific, and also a stranglehold on the west coast of North and Central and South America.

We know also that Germany and Japan are conducting their military and naval operations in accordance with a joint plan. That plan considers all peoples and nations which are not helping the Axis powers as common enemies of each and every one of the Axis powers.

That is their simple and obvious grand strategy. That is why the American people must realize that it can be matched only with similar grand strategy.

We must realize, for example, that Japanese successes against the United States in the Pacific are helpful to German operations in Libya; that any German success against the Caucasus is inevitably an assistance to Japan in her operations against the Dutch East Indies; that a German attack against Algiers or Morocco opens the way to a German attack against South America and the Canal.

On the other side of the picture, we must learn also to know that guerrilla warfare against the Germans in, let us say, Serbia, or Norway, helps us; that a successful Russian offensive against the Germans helps us; and that British success on land or sea in any part of the world strengthens our hands.

Remember always that Germany and Italy, regardless of any formal declaration of war, consider themselves at war with the United States at this moment just as much as they consider themselves at war with Britain or Russia. And Germany puts all the other Republics of the Americas into the same category of enemies. The people of our sister Republics of this Hemisphere can be honored by that fact.

The true goal we seek is far above and beyond the ugly field of battle. When we resort to force, as now we must, we are determined that this force shall be directed toward ultimate good as well as against immediate evil. We Americans are not destroyers — we are builders.

We are now in the midst of a war, not for conquest, not for vengeance, but for a world in which this nation, and all that this nation represents, will be safe for our children. We expect to eliminate the danger from Japan, but it would serve us ill if we accomplished that and found that the rest of the world was dominated by Hitler and Mussolini.

So, we are going to win the war and we are going to win the peace that follows.

And in the difficult hours of this day — and through dark days that may be yet to come — we will know that the vast majority of the members of the human race are on our side. Many of them are fighting with us. All of them are praying for us. For, in representing our cause, we represent theirs as well — our hope and their hope for liberty under God.

ANNUAL MESSAGE TO CONGRESS
January 6, 1942

In a fighting mood, the President outlined the seemingly impossible goals which he was asking of the American productive plant, and called for "all-out" effort by every American.

In fulfilling my duty to report upon the state of the Union I am proud to say to you that the spirit of the American people was never higher than it is today — the Union was never more closely knit together — this country was never more deeply determined to face the solemn tasks before it.

The response of the American people has been instantaneous. It will be sustained until our security is assured.

Exactly one year ago today I said to this Congress: "When the dictators are ready to make war upon us, they will not wait for an act of war on our part. . . . They — not we — will choose the time and the place and the method of their attack."

We now know their choice of the time: a peaceful Sunday morning — December 7, 1941.

We know their choice of the place: an American outpost in the Pacific.

We know their choice of the method: the method of Hitler himself.

Japan's scheme of conquest goes back half a century. It was not merely a policy of seeking living room: it was a plan which included the subjugation of all the peoples in the Far East and in the islands of the Pacific, and the domination of that ocean by Japanese military and naval control of the western coasts of North, Central and South America.

The development of this ambitious conspiracy was marked by the war against China in 1894; the subsequent occupation of Korea; the war against Russia in 1904; the illegal fortification of the mandated Pacific islands following 1920; the seizure of Manchuria in 1931; and the invasion of China in 1937.

A similar policy of criminal conquest was adopted by Italy. The Fascists first revealed their imperial designs in Libya and Tripoli. in 1935 they seized Abyssinia. Their goal was the domination of all North Africa, Egypt, parts of France, and the entire Mediterranean world.

But the dreams of empire of the Japanese and Fascist leaders were modest in comparison with the gargantuan aspirations of Hitler and his

Nazis. Even before they came to power in 1933, their plans for conquest had been drawn. Those plans provided for ultimate domination, not of any one section of the world but of the whole earth and all the oceans on it.

With Hitler's formation of the Berlin-Rome-Tokyo alliance, all of these plans of conquest became a single plan. Under this, in addition to her own schemes of conquest, Japan's role was to cut off our supply of weapons of war to Britain, Russia, and China — weapons which increasingly were speeding the day of Hitler's doom. The act of Japan at Pearl Harbor was intended to stun us — to terrify us to such an extent that we would divert our industrial and military strength to the Pacific area or even to our own continental defense.

The plan failed in its purpose. We have not been stunned. We have not been terrified or confused. This reassembling of the Seventy-seventh Congress is proof of that; for the mood of quiet, grim resolution which here prevails bodes ill for those who conspired and collaborated to murder world peace.

That mood is stronger than any mere desire for revenge. It expresses the will of the American people to make very certain that the world will never so suffer again.

Admittedly, we have been faced with hard choices. It was bitter, for example, not to be able to relieve the heroic defenders of Wake Island. It was bitter for us not to be able to land a million men and a thousand ships in the Philippine Islands.

But this adds only to our determination to see to it that the Stars and Stripes will fly again over Wake and Guam; and that the brave people of the Philippines will be rid of Japanese imperialism, and will live in freedom, security, and independence.

Powerful and offensive actions must and will be taken in proper time. The consolidations of the United Nations' total war effort against our common enemies is being achieved.

That is the purpose of conferences which have been held during the past two weeks in Washington, in Moscow, and in Chungking. That is the primary objective of the declaration of solidarity signed in Washington on January 1st, 1942, by 26 nations united against the Axis powers.

Difficult choices may have to be made in the months to come. We will not shrink from such decisions. We and those united with us will make those decisions with courage and determination.

Plans have been laid here and in the other capitals for coordinated and cooperative action by all the United Nations — military action and economic action. Already we have established unified command of land, sea, and air forces in the southwestern Pacific theater of war. There will be a continuation of conferences and consultations among military staffs, so that the plans and operations of each will fit into a general strategy designed to crush the enemy. We shall not fight isolated wars — each nation going its own way. These 26 nations are united — not in spirit and determination alone but in the broad conduct of the war in all its phases.

For the first time since the Japanese and the Fascists and the Nazis started along their blood-stained course of conquest they now face the fact that superior forces are assembling aginst them. Gone forever are the days when the aggressors could attack and destroy their victims one by one without unity of resistance. We of the United Nations will so dispose of our forces that we can strike at the common enemy wherever the greatest damage can be done.

The militarists in Berlin and Tokyo started this war. But the massed, angered forces of common humanity will finish it.

Destruction of the material and spiritual centers of civilization — this has been and still is the purpose of Hitler and his Italian and Japanese chessmen. They would wreck the power of the British Commonwealth and Russia and China and the Netherlands — and then combine all their forces to achieve their ultimate goal, the conquest of the United States.

They know that victory for us means victory for freedom.

They know that victory for us means victory for the institution of democracy — the ideal of the family, the simple principles of common decency and humanity.

They know that victory for us means victory for religion.

And they could not tolerate that. the world is too small to provide adequate "living room" for both Hitler and God. In proof of that, the Nazis have now announced their plan for enforcing their new German, pagan religion throughout the world — the plan by which the Holy Bible and the Cross of Mercy would be displaced by MEIN KAMPF and the swastika and the naked sword.

Our own objectives are clear: the objective of smashing the militarism imposed by the warlords upon their enslaved peoples — the objective of liberating the subjugated nations — the objective of establishing and securing freedom of speech, freedom of religion, freedom from want, and freedom from fear everywhere in the world.

We shall not stop short of these objectives — nor shall we be satisfied merely to gain them and then call it a day. I know that I speak for the American people — and I have good reason to believe I speak also for all the other peoples who fight with us — when I say that this time we are determined not only to win the war but also to maintain the security of the peace which will follow.

But modern methods of warfare make it a task not only of shooting and fighting, but an even more urgent one of working and producing.

Victory requires the actual weapons of war and the means of transporting them to a dozen points of combat.

It will not be sufficient for us and the other United Nations to produce a slightly superior supply of munitions to that of Germany, Japan, Italy, and the stolen industries in the countries which they have overrun.

The superiority of the United Nations in munitions and ships must be overwhelming — so overwhelming that the Axis nations can never hope to catch up with it. In order to attain this overwhelming superiority the United Nations must build planes and tanks and guns and ships to the utmost limit of our national capacity. We have the ability and capacity to produce arms not only for our own forces but also for the armies, navies, and air forces fighting on our side.

And our overwhelming superiority of armament must be adequate to put weapons of war at the proper time into the hands of those men in the conquered nations, who stand ready to seize the first opportunity to revolt against their German and Japanese aggressors, and against the traitors in their own ranks, known by the already infamous name of "Quislings." As we get guns to the patriots in those lands, they too will fire shots heard 'round the world.

This production of ours in the United States must be raised far above its present levels, even though it will mean the dislocation of the lives and occupations of millions of our own people. We must raise our signts all along the production-line. Let no man say it cannot be done. It must be done — and we have undertaken to do it.

I have just sent a letter of directive to the appropriate departments and agencies of our Government, ordering that immediate steps be taken:

1. To increase our production rate of airplanes so rapidly that in this year, 1942, we shall produce 60,000 planes, 10,000 more than the goal set a year and a half ago. This includes 45,000 combat planes — bombers, dive bombers, pursuit planes. The rate of increase will be continued, so that next year, 1943, we shall produce 125,000 planes, including 100,000 combat planes.

2. To increase our production rate of tanks so rapidly that in this year, 1942, we shall produce 45,000 tanks; and to continue that increase so that next year, 1943, we shall produce 75,000 tanks.

3. To increase our production rate of anti-aircraft guns so rapidly that in this year, 1942, we shall produce 20,000 of them; and to continue that increase, so that next year, 1943, we shall produce 35,000 anti-aircraft guns.

4. To increase our production rate of merchant ships so rapidly that in this year, 1942, we shall build 8,000,000 deadweight tons as compared with a 1941 production of 1,100,000. We shall continue that increase so that next year, 1943, we shall build 10,000,000 tons.

These figures and similar figures for a multitude of other implementsof war will give the Japanese and Nazis a little idea of just what they accomplished in the attack on Pearl Harbor.

Our task is hard—our task is unprecedented – and the time is short. We must strain every existing armament-producing facility to the utmost. We must convert every available plant and tool to war production. That goes all the way from the greatest plants to the smallest – from the huge automobile industry to the village machine shop.

Production for war is based on men and women – the human hands and brains which collectively we call labor. Our workers stand ready to work long hours; to turn out more in a day's work; to keep the wheels turning and the fires burning 24 hours a day and 7 days a week. They realize well that on the speed and efficiency of their work depend the lives of their sons and their brothers on the fighting fronts.

Production for war is based on metals and raw materials – steel, copper, rubber, aluminum, zinc, tin. Greater and greater quantities of them will have to be diverted to war purposes. Civilian use of them will have to be cut further and still further– and, in many cases, completely eliminated.

War costs money. So far, we have hardly even begun to pay for it. We have devoted only 15 per cent of our national income to our national defense. As will appear in my budget message tomorrow, our war program for the coming fiscal year will cost 56 billion dollars, or, in other words, more than one-half of the estimated annual national income. This means taxes and bonds, and bonds and taxes. It means cutting luxuries and other non-essentials. In a word, it means, an "all-out" war by individual effort and family effort in a united country.

Only this all-out scale of production will hasten the ultimate all-out victory. Speed will count. Lost ground can always be regained – lost time never. Speed will save lives; speed will save this Nation which is in peril; speed will save our freedom and civilization – and slowness has never been an American characteristic.

As the United States goes into its full stride, we must always be on guard against misconceptions which will arise naturally or which will be planted among us by our enemies.

We must guard against complacency. We must not underrate the enemy. He is powerful and cunning – and cruel and ruthless. He will stop at nothing which gives him a chance to kill and to destroy. He has trained his people to believe that their highest perfection is achieved by waging war. For many years he has prepared for this very conflict –

planning, plotting, training, arming, fighting. We have already tasted defeat. We may suffer further setbacks. We must face the fact of a hard war, a long war, a bloody war, a costly war.

We must, on the other hand, guard against defeatism. That has been one of the chief weapons of Hitler's propaganda machine – used time and again with deadly results. It will not be used successfully on the American people.

We must guard against divisions among ourselves and among all the other United Nations. We must be particularly vigilant against racial discrimination in any of its ugly forms. Hitler will try again to breed mistrust and suspicion between one individual and another, one group and another, one race and another, one government and another. He will try to use the same technique of falsehood and rumor-mongering with which he divided France from Britain. He is trying to do this with us even now. But he will find a unity of will and purpose against him, which will persevere until the destruction of all his black designs upon the freedom and safety of the people of the world.

We cannot wage this war in a defensive spirit. As our power and our resources are fully mobilized, we shall carry the attack against the enemy – we shall hit him and hit him again wherever and whenever we can reach him.

We must keep him far from our shores, for we intend to bring this battle to him on his own home grounds.

American armed forces must be used at any place in all the world where it seems advisable to engage the forces of the enemy. In some cases these operations will be defensive, in order to protect key positions. In other cases, these operations will be offensive, in order to strike at the common enemy, with a view to his complete encirclement and eventual total defeat.

American armed forces will operate at many points in the Far East.

American armed forces will be on all the oceans – helping to guard the essential communications which are vital to the United Nations.

American land and air and sea forces will take stations in the British Isles – which constitute an essential fortress in this world struggle.

American armed forces will help to protect this hemisphere – and also bases outside this hemisphere which could be used for an attack on the Americas.

If any of our enemies from Europe or from Asia attempt long-range raids by "Suicide" squadrons of bombing planes, they will do so only in the hope of terrorizing our people and disrupting our morale. Our people are not afraid of that. We know that we may have to pay a heavy price for freedom. We will pay this price with a will. Whatever the price, it is a thousand times worth it. No matter what our enemies in their desperation may attempt to do to us — we will say, as the people of London have said, "We can take it." And what's more, we can give it back — and we will give it back — with compound interest.

When our enemies challenged our country to stand up and fight, they challenged each and every one of us. And each and every one of us has accepted the challenge — for himself and for the Nation.

There were only some 400 United States Marines who in the heroic and historic defense of Wake Island inflicted such great losses on the enemy. Some of those men were killed in action; and others are now prisoners of war. When the survivors of that great fight are liberated and restored to their homes, they will learn that one hundred and thirty million of their fellow citizens have been inspired to render their own full share of service and sacrifice.

Our men on the fighting fronts have already proved that Americans today are just as rugged and just as tough as any of the heroes whose exploits we celebrate on the Fourth of July.

Many people ask, "When will this war end?" There is only one answer to that. It will end just as soon as we make it end, by our combined efforts, our combined strength, our combined determination to fight through and work through until the end — the end of militarism in Germany and Italy and Japan. Most certainly we shall not settle for less.

That is the spirit in which discussions have been conducted during the visit of the British Prime Minister to Washington. Mr. Churchill and I understand each other, our motives and our purposes. Together, during the past two weeks, we have faced squarely the major military and economic problems of this greatest world war.

All in our Nation have been cheered by Mr. Churchill's visit. We have been deeply stirred by his great message to us. We wish him a safe return to his home. He is welcome in our midst, now and in days to come.

We are fighting on the same side with the British people, who fought alone for long, terrible months and withstood the enemy with fortitude and tenacity and skill.

We are fighting on the same side with the Russian people who have seen the Nazi hordes swarm up to the very gates of Moscow adn who with almost superhuman will and courage, have forced the invaders back into retreat.

We are fighting on the same side as the brave people of China who for four and a half long years have withstood bombs and starvation and have whipped the invaders time and again in spite of superior Japanese equipment and arms.

We are fighting on the same side as the indomitable Dutch.

We are fighting on the same side as all the other governments in exile, whom Hitler and all his armies and all his Gestapo have not been able to conquer.

But we of the United Nations are not making all of this sacrifice of human effort and human lives to return to the kind of world we had after the last world war.

We are fighting today for security, for progress, and for peace, not only for ourselves but for all men, not only for one generation but for all generations. We are fighting to cleanse the world of ancient evils, ancient ills.

Our enemies are guided by brutal cynicism, by unholy contempt for the human race. We are inspired by a faith which goes back all the years to the first chapter of the Book of Genesis: "God created man in His own image."

We on our side are striving to be true to that divine heritage. We are fighting, as our fathers have fought, to uphold the doctrine that all men are equal in the sight of God. Those on the other side are fighting to destroy this deep belief and to create a world in their own image — a world of tyranny and cruelty and serfdom.

That is the conflict that day and night now pervades our lives. No compromise can end that conflict. There never has been — there never can be — successful compromise between good and evil. Only total victory can reward the champions of tolerance and decency and freedom and faith.

FIRESIDE CHAT ON INFLATION AND TAXES
September 7, 1943

*The President asked the American people to support his
call to Congress to control inflation and finance the war
by increased taxes. He created a sensation by his request
for a $25,000 net income limit.*

I wish that all the American people could read all the citations for
various medals recommended for our soldiers, sailors and marines.
I am picking out one of these citations which tells of the accomplish-
ments of Lieutenant John James Powers, United States Navy, during
three days of the battles with Japanese forces in the Coral Sea.

During the first two days, Lieutenant Powers, flying a dive bomber
in the face of blasting enemy anti-aircraft fire, demolished one large
enemy gunboat, put another gunboat out of commission, severely dam-
aged an aircraft tender and a twenty thousand ton transport, and scored
a direct hit on an aircraft carrier which burst into flames and sank
soon after.

The official citation describes the morning of the third day of battle. As the pilots of his squadron left the ready room to man their
planes, Lieutenant Powers said to them, "Remember, the folks back
home are counting on us. I am going to get a hit if I have to lay it on
their flight deck."

He led this section down to the target from an altitude of 18,000
feet, through a wall of bursting anti-aircraft shells and swarms of
enemy planes. He dived almost to the very deck of the enemy carrier,
and did not release his bomb until he was sure of a direct hit. He was
last seen attempting recovery from his dive at the extremely low altitude of two hundred feet, amid a terrific barrage of shell and bomb
fragments, smoke, flame and debris from the stricken vessel. His own
plane was destroyed by the explosion of his own bomb. But he had made
good his promise to "lay it on the flight deck."

I have received a recommendation from the Secretary of the Navy
that Lieutenant James Powers, of New York City, missing in action, be
awarded the Medal of Honor. I hereby and now make this award.

You and I are "the folks back home" for whose protection Lieutenant Powers fought and repeatedly risked his life. He said that we
counted on him and his men. We did not count in vain. But have not
those men a right to be counting on us? How are we playing our part
"back home" in winning this war? The answer is that we are not doing enough.

Today I sent a message to the Congress, pointing out the overwhelming urgency of the serious domestic economic crisis with which we are threatened, and others call it "inflation," which is a vague sort of term, and others call it a "rise in the cost of living," which is much more easily understood by most families.

That phrase, "the cost of living," means essentially what a dollar can buy.

From January 1, 1941 to May of this year, the cost of living went up about 15 percent. At that point we undertook to freeze the cost of living. But we could not do a complete job of it, because the Congressional authority at the time exempted a large part of farm products used for food and for making clothing; though several weeks before, I had asked the Congress for legislation to stabilize all farm prices.

At that time I had told the Congress that there were seven elements in our national economy, all of which had to be controlled; and that if any one essential element remained exempt, the cost of living could not be held down.

On only two of these points — both of them vital however – did I call for Congressional action. These were: first, taxation; and, second, the stabilization of all farm prices at parity.

"Parity" is a standard for the maintneance of good farm prices. It was established as our national policy in 1933. It means that the farmer and the city worker are on the same relative ratio with each other in purchasing power as they were during a period some thirty years ago — at a time when the farmer had a satisfactory purchasing power. One hundred percent parity, therefore, has been accepted by farmers as the fair standard for their prices.

Last January, however, the Congress passed a law forbidding ceilings on farm prices below 110 percent of parity on some commodities. On other commodities the ceiling was even higher, so that the average possible ceiling is now about 116 percent of parity for agricultural products as a whole.

This act of favoritism for one particular group in the community increased the cost of food to everybody — not only to the workers in the city or in the munitions plants, and their families, but also to the families of the farmers themselves.

Since last May, ceilings have been set on nearly all commodities, rents and services, except the exempted farm products. Installment buying has been effectively controlled.

Wages in certain key industries have been stabilized on the basis of the present cost of living.

It is obvious, however, that if the cost of food continues to go up, as it is doing at present, the wage earner, particularly in the lower brackets, will have a right to an increase in his wages. That would be essential justice and a practical necessity.

Our experience with the control of other prices during the past few months has brought out one important fact — the rising cost of living can be controlled, providing all elements making up the cost of living are controlled at the same time. We know that parity prices for farm products not now controlled will not put up the cost of living more than a very small amount; but that if we must go up to an average of 116 percent of parity for food and other farm products — which is necessary at present under the Emergency Price Control Act before we can control all farm prices — the cost of living will get well out of hand. We are face to face with this danger today. Let us meet it and remove it.

I realize that it may seem out of proportion to you to be worrying about these economic problems at a time like this when we are all deeply concerned about the news from far distant fields of battle. But I give you the solemn assurance that failure to solve this problem here at home — and to solve it now — will make more difficult the winning of this war.

If the vicious spiral of inflation ever gets under way, the whole economic system will stagger. Prices and wages will go up so rapidly that the entire production program will be endangered. The cost of the war, paid by taxpayers, will jump beyond all present calculations. It will mean an uncontrollable rise in prices and in wages which can result in raising the over-all cost of living as high as another 20 percent. That would mean that the purchasing power of every dollar you have in your pay envelope, or in the bank, or included in your insurance policy or your pension, would be reduced to about eighty cents. I need not tell you that this would have a demoralizing effect on our people, soldiers, and civilians alike.

Over-all stabilization of prices, salaries, wages and profits is necessary to the continued increasing production of planes and tanks and ships and guns.

In my message today I have told the Congress that this must be done quickly. If we wait for two or three or four or six months it may well be too late.

I have told the Congress that the Administration can not hold the actual cost of food and clothing down to the present level beyond October first.

Therefore, I have asked the Congress to pass legislation under which the President would be specifically authorized to stabilize the cost of living, including the price of all farm commodities. The purpose should be to hold farm prices at parity, or at level of a recent date, whichever is higher. The purpose should also be to keep wages at a point stabilized with today's cost of living. Both must be regulated at the same time; and neither can or should be regulated without the other.

At the same time that farm prices are stabilized, I will stabilize wages.

This is plain justice – and plain common sense.

I have asked the Congress to take this action by the first of October. We must now act with the dispatch which the stern necessities of war require.

I have told the Congress that inaction on their part by that date will leave me with an inescapable responsibility to the people of this country to see to it that the war effort is no longer imperiled by the threat of economic chaos.

As I said in my message to the Congress:

In the event that the Congress should fail to act, and act adequately, I shall accept the responsibility, and I will act.

The President has the powers, under the Constitution and under Congressional Acts, to take measures necessary to avert a disaster which would interfere with the winning of the war.

I have given the most thoughtful consideration to meeting this issue without further reference to the Congress. I have determined, however, on this vital matter to consult with the Congress.

There may be those who will say that, if the situation is as grave as I have stated it to be, I should use my powers and act now. I can only say that I have decided that the course of conduct which I am following in this case is consistent with my sense of responsibility as President in time of war, and with my deep and unalterable devotion to the processes of democracy.

The responsibilities of the President in war time to protect the Nations are very grave. This total war, with our fighting fronts all over the world, makes the use of executive power far more essential than in any previous war.

If we were invaded, the people of this country would expect the President to use any and all means to repel the invader.

The Revolution and the War between the States was fought on our own soil but today this war will be won or lost on other continents and remote seas. I cannot tell what powers may have to be exercised in order to win this war.

The American people can be sure that I will use my powers with a full sense of responsibility to the Constitution and to my country. The American people can also be sure that I shall not hesitate to use every power vested in me to accomplish the defeat of our enemies in any part of the world where our own safety demands such defeat.

When the war is won, the powers under which I act will automatical-
ly revert to the people – to whom they belong.

I think I know the American farmers. I know that they are as whole-
hearted in their patriotism as any other group. They have suffered
from the constant fluctuations of farm prices – occasionally too high,
more often too low. Nobody knows better than farmers the disastrous
effects of war time inflationary booms and post-war deflationary
panics.

I have today suggested that the Congress make our agricultural
economy more stable. I have recommended that in addition to putting
ceilings on all farm products now, we also place a definite floor under
those prices for a period beginning now, continuing through the war, and
for as long as necessary after the war. In this way we will be able to
avoid the collapse of farm prices which happened after the last war.
The farmers must be assured of a fair minimum price during the readjustment period which will follow the excessive world food demands
which now prevail.

We must have some floor under farm prices, as we have under
wages, if we are to avoid the dangers of a post-war inflation on the
one hand, or the catastrophe of a crash in farm prices and wages, on
the other.

Today I have also advised the Congress of the importance of speeding up the passage of the tax bill. The Federal Treasury is losing
millions of dollars a day because the bill has not yet been passed.
Taxation is the only practical way of preventing the incomes and profits of individuals and corporations from getting too high.

I have told the Congress once more that all net individual incomes,
after payment of all taxes, should be limited effectively by further
taxation to a minimum net income of $25,000 a year. And it is equally
important that corporate profits should not exceed a reasonable amount
in any case.

The nation must have more money to run the War. People must
stop spending for luxuries. Our country needs a far greater share of
our incomes.

For this is a global war and it will cost this nation nearly one
hundred billion dollars in 1943.

In that global war there are now four main areas of combat; and
I should like to speak briefly of them, not in the order of importance,
for all of them are vital and all of them inter-related.

(1) The Russian front. Here the Germans are still unable to gain the
smashing victory which, almost a year ago, Hitler announced he had
already achieved. Germany has been able to capture important Russian
territory. Nevertheless, Hitler has been unable to destroy a single

Russian Army; and this, you may be sure, has been and still is, his main objective. Millions of German troops seem doomed to spend another cruel and bitter winter on the Russian front. The Russians are killing more Nazis, and destroying more airplanes and tanks than are being smashed on any other front. They are fighting not only bravely but brilliantly. In spite of any setbacks, Russia will hold out, and with the help of her Allies will ultimately drive every Nazi from her soil.

(2) The Pacific Area. This area must be grouped together as a whole — every part of it, land and sea. We have stopped one major Japanese offensive; and have inflicted heavy losses on their fleet. But they still possess great strength; they seek to keep the initiative; and they will undoubtedly strike hard again. We must not overrate the importance of our successes in the Solomon Islands, though we may be proud of the skill with which these local operations were conducted. At the same time, we need not under-rate the significance of our victory at Midway. There we stopped the major Japanese offensive.

(3) In the Mediterranean and the Middle East area the British, together with the South Africans, Australians, New Zealanders, Indian troops and others of the United Nations, including ourselves, are fighting a desperate battle with the Germans and Italians. The Axis powers are fighting to gain control of that area, dominate the Mediterranean and Indian Ocean, and gain contact with the Japanese Navy. The battle is now joined. We are well aware of our danger, but we are hopeful of the outcome.

(4) The European area. Here the aim is an offensive against Germany. There are at least a dozen different points at which attacks can be launched. You, of course, do not expect me to give details of future plans, but you can rest assured that preparations are being made here and in Britain toward this purpose. The power of Germany must be broken on the battlefields of Europe.

Various people urge that we concentrate our forces on one or another of these four areas, although no one suggests that any one of the four areas should be abandoned. Certainly, it could not be seriously urged that we abandon aid to Russia, or surrender all the Pacific to Japan, or the Mediterranean and Middle East to Germany, or give up an offensive against Germany. The American people may be sure that we shall neglect none of the four great theatres of war.

Certain vital military decisions have been made. In due time you will know what these decisions are — and so will our enemies. I can say now that all of these decisions are directed toward taking the offensive.

Today, exactly one year and nine months after Pearl Harbor, we have sent overseas three times more men than we transported to France in the first nine months of the first World War. We have done this in spite of greater danger and fewer ships. And every week sees a gain in the actual number of American men and weapons in the fighting areas. These reinforcements in men and munitions will continue to go forward.

This war will finally be won by the coordination of all the armies, navies and air forces of the United Nations operating in unison against our enemies.

This will require vast assemblies of weapons and men at all the vital points of attack. We and our allies have worked for years to achieve superiority in weapons. We have no doubts about the superiority of our men. We glory in the individual exploits of our soldiers, our sailors, our marines, our merchant seamen. Lieutenant John James Powers was one of these – and there are thousands of others in the forces of the United States.

Several thousand Americans have met death in battle. Other thousands will lose their lives. But many millions stand ready to step into their places – to engage in a struggle to the very death. For they know that the enemy is determined to destroy us, our homes and our institutions – that in this war it is kill or be killed.

Battles are not won by soldiers or sailors who think first of their own personal safety. And wars are not won by people who are concerned primarily with their own comfort, their own convenience, their own pocketbooks.

We Americans of today bear the gravest of responsibilities. All of the United Nations share them.

All of us here at home are being tested – for our fortitude, for our selfless devotion to our country and our cause.

This is the toughest war of all time. We need not leave it to historians of the future to answer the question whether we are tough enough to meet this unprecedented challenge. We can give that answer now. The answer is "yes."

ANNUAL MESSAGE TO CONGRESS
January 11, 1944

Shortly after his comment that "Dr. New Deal" had given way to "Dr. Win the War" President Roosevelt gave what was undoubtedly the most radical speech of his life. Unable to deliver it to Congress in person, having come down with the flu, he went on radio to address the American people. What he called for amounted to a Third New Deal, which, had he lived, he might have pressed for after the war Congress, however, was unresponsive to the appeal

This Nation in the past two years has become an active partner in the world's greatest war against human slavery.

We have joined with like-minded people in order to defend ourselves in a world that has been gravely threatened with gangster rule.

But I do not think that any of us Americans can be content with mere survival. Sacrifices that we and our Allies are making impose upon us all a sacred obligation to see to it that out of this war we and our children will gain something better than mere survival.

We are united in determination that this war shall not be followed by another interim which leads to new disaster — that we shall not repeat the tragic errors of ostrich isolationism — that we shall not repeat the excesses of the wild twenties when this Nation went for a joy-ride on a roller coaster which ended in a tragic crash.

When Mr. Hull went to Moscow in October, and when I went to Cairo and Teheran in November, we knew that we were in agreement with our Allies in our common determination to fight and win this war. But there were many vital questions concerning the future peace, and they were discussed in an atmosphere of complete candor and harmony.

In the last war such discussions, such meetings, did not even begin until the shooting had stopped and the delegates began to assemble at the peace table. There had been no previous opportunities for man-to-man discussions which lead to meetings of minds. The result was a peace which was not a peace.

That was a mistake which we are not repeating in this war.

And right here I want to address a word or two to some suspicious souls who are fearful that Mr. Hull or I have made "commitments" for the future which might pledge this Nation to secret treaties, or to enacting the role of Santa Claus.

To such suspicious souls — using a polite terminology — I wish to say that Mr. Churchill, and Marshal Stalin, and Generalissimo Chiang Kai-shek are all thoroughly conversant with the provisions of our Constitution. And so is Mr. Hull. And So am I.

Of course we made some commitments. We most certainly committed ourselves to very large and very specific military plans which require the use of all allied forces to bring about the defeat of our enemies at the earliest possible time.

But there were no secret treaties or political or financial commitments.

The one supreme objective for the future, which we discussed for each nation individually, and for all the United Nations, can be summed up in one word: Security.

And that means not only physical security which provides safety from attacks by aggressors. It means also economic security, social security, moral security — in a family of nations.

In the plain down-to-earth talks that I had with the Generalissimo and Marshal Stalin and Prime Minister Churchill, it was abundantly clear that they are all most deeply interested in the resumption of peaceful progress by their own peoples — progress toward a better life. All our Allies want freedom to develop their lands and resources, to build up industry, to increase education and individual opportunity, and to raise standards of living.

All our Allies have learned by bitter experience that real development will not be possible if they are to be diverted from their purpose by repeated wars — or even threats of war.

China and Russia are truly united with Britain and America in recognition of this essential fact:

The best interests of each nation, large and small, demand that all freedom-loving nations shall join together in a just and durable system of peace. In the present world situation, evidenced by the actions of Germany, Italy and Japan, unquestioned military control over disturbers of the peace is as necessary among nations as it is among citizens in a community. And an equally basic essential to peace is a decent standard of living for all individual men and women and children in all nations. Freedom from fear is eternally linked with freedom from want.

There are people who burrow through our Nation like unseeing moles, and attempt to spread the suspicion that if other nations are encouraged to raise their standards of living, our own American standard of living must of necessity be depressed.

The fact is the very contrary. It has been shown time and again that if the standard of living of any country goes up, so does its purchasing power — and that such a rise encourages a better standard of living in neighboring countries with whom it trades. That is just plain common sense — and it is the kind of plain common sense that provided the basis for our discussions at Moscow, Cairo and Teheran.

Returning from my journeyings, I must confess to a sense of "let-down" when I found many evidences of faulty perspectives here in Washington. The faulty perspective consists in over-emphasizing lesser problems and thereby under-emphasizing the first and greatest problem.

The overwhelming majority of our people have met the demands of this war with magnificent courage and understanding. They have accepted inconveniences; they have accepted hardships; they have accepted tragic sacrifices. And they are ready and eager to make whatever further contributions are needed to win the war as quickly as possible — if only they are given the chance to know what is required of them.

However, while the majority goes on about its great work without compalint, a noisy minority maintains an uproar of demands for special favors for special groups. There are pests who swarm through the lobbies of the Congress and the cocktail bars of Washington, representing these special groups as opposed to the basic interests of the nation as a whole. They have come to look upon the war primarily as a chance to make profits for themselves at the expense of their neighbors — profits in money or in terms of political or social preferment.

Such selfish agitation can be highly dangerous in wartime. It creates confusion. It damages morale. It hampers our national effort. It muddies the waters and therefore prolongs the war.

If we analyze American history impartially, we cannot escape the fact that in our past we have not always forgotten individual and selfish and partisan interests in time of war — we have not always been united in purpose and direction. We cannot overlook the serious dissensions and the lack of unity in our war of the Revolution, in our War of 1812, or in our War Between the States, when the survival of the Union itself was at stake.

In the first World War we came closer to national unity than in any previous war. But that war lasted only a year and a half, and increasing signs of disunity began to appear during the final months of the conflict.

In this war, we have been compelled to learn how interdependent upon each other are all groups and sections of the population of America.

Increased food costs, for example, will bring new demands for wage increases from all war workers, which will in turn raise all prices of all things including those things which the farmers themselves have to buy. Increased wages or prices will each in turn produce the same results. They all have a particularly disastrous result on all fixed income groups.

And I hope you will remember that all of us in this Government represent the fixed income group just as much as we represent business owners, workers and farmers. This group of fixed-income people include: teachers, clergy, policemen, firemen, widows and minors on fixed incomes, wives and dependents of our soldiers and sailors, and old age pensioners. They and their families add up to one quarter of our one hundred and thirty million people. They have few or no high pressure representatives at the Capitol. In a period of gross inflation they would be the worst sufferers.

If ever there was a time to subordinate individual or group selfishness to the national good, that time is now. Disunity at home — bickerings, self-seeking partisanship, stoppages of work, inflation, business as usual, politics as usual, luxury as usual — these are the influences which can undermine the morale of the brave men ready to die at the front for us here.

Those who are doing most of the complaining are not deliberately striving to sabotage the national war effort. They are laboring under the delusion that the time is past when we must make prodigious sacrifices — that the war is already won and we can begin to slacken off. But the dangerous folly of that point of view can be measured by the distance that separates our troops from their ultimate objectives in Berlin and Tokyo — and by the sum of all the perils that lie along the way.

Over-confidence and complacency are among our deadliest enemies. Last Spring — after notable victories at Stalingrad and in Tunisia and against the U-boats on the high seas — over-confidence became so pronounced that war production fell off. In two months, June and Junly, 1943, more than a thousand airplanes that could have been made and should have been made were not made. Those who failed to make them were not on strike. They were merely saying, "The war's in the bag — so let's relax."

That attitude on the part of anyone — Government or management or labor — can lengthen this war. It can kill American boys.

Let us remember the lessons of 1918. In the Summer of that year the tide turned in favor of the Allies. But this Government did not relax. In fact, our national effort was stepped up. In August, 1918, the draft age limits were broadened from 21-31 to 18-45. The President called for "force to the utmost," and his call was heeded. And in November, only three months later, Germany surrendered.

That is the way to fight and win a war — all out — and not with half-an-eye on the battlefronts abroad and the other eye-and-a-half on personal, selfish, or political interests here at home.

Therefore, in order to concentrate all our energies and resources on winning the war, and to maintain a fair and stable economy at home, I recommend that the Congress adopt:

(1) A realistic tax law – which will tax all unreasonable profits, both individual and corporate, and recuce the ultimate cost of the war to our sons and daughters. The tax bill now under consideration by the Congress does not begin to meet this test.

(2) A continuation of the law for the renegotiation of war contracts – which will prevent exorbitant profits and assure fair prices to the Government. For two long years I have pleaded with the Congress to take undue profits out of the war.

(3) A cost of food law – which will enable the Government (a) to place a reasonable floor under the prices the farmer may expect for his production; and (b) to place a ceiling on the prices a consumer will have to pay for the food he buys. This should apply to necessities only; and will require public funds to carry out. It will cost in appropriations about one percent of the present annual cost of the war.

(4) Early reenactment of the stabilization statute of October 1942. This expires June 30th, 1944, and if it is not extended well in advance, the country might just as well expect price chaos by Summer.

We cannot have stabilization by wishful thinking. We must take positive action to maintain the integrity of the American dollar.

(5) A national service law – which, for the duration of the war, will prevent strikes, and, with certain appropriate exceptions, will make available for war production or for any other essential services every able-bodied adult in this nation.

These five measures together form a just and equitable whole. I would not recommend a national service law unless the other laws were passed to keep down the cost of living, to share equitably the burdens of taxation, to hold the stabilization line, and to prevent undue profits.

The Federal Government already has the basic power to draft capital and property of all kinds for war purposes on a basis of just compensation.

As you know, I have for three years hesitated to recommend a national service act. Today, however, I am convinced of its necessity. Although I believe that we and our Allies can win the war without such a measure, I am certain that nothing less than total mobilization of all our resources of manpower and capital will guarantee an earlier victory and reduce the toll of suffering and sorrow and blood.

I have received a joint recommendation for this law from the heads of the War Department, the Navy Department and the Maritime Commission. These are the men who bear responsibility for the procurement of the necessary arms and equipment, and for the successful prosecution of the war in the field. They say:

"When the very life of the nation is in peril the responsibility for service is common to all men and women. In such a time there can be no discrimination between the men and women who are assigned by the Government to its defense at the battlefront and the men and women assigned to producing the vital materials essential to successful military operations. A prompt enactment of a National Service Law would be merely an expression of the universality of this responsibility."

I believe the country will agree that those statements are the solemn truth.

National service is the most democratic way to wage a war. Like selective service for the armed forces, it rests on the obligation of each citizen to serve his nation to his utmost where he is best qualified.

It does not mean reduction in wages. It does not mean loss of retirement and seniority rights and benefits. It does not mean that any substantial numbers of war workers will be disturbed in their present jobs. Let these facts be wholly clear.

Experience in other democratic nations at war — Britain, Canada, Australia and New Zealand — has shown that the very existence of national service makes unnecessary the widespread use of compulsory power. National service has proven to be a unifying moral force — based on an equal and comprehensive legal obligation of all people in a nation at war.

There are millions of American men and women who are not in this war at all. It is not because they do not want to be in it. But they want to know where they can best do their share. National service provides that direction. It will be a means by which every man and woman can find that inner satisfaction which comes from making the fullest possible contribution to victory.

I know that all civilian war workers will be glad to be able to say many years hence to their grandchildren: "Yes, I, too, was in service in the great war. I was on duty in an airplane factory, and I helped make hundreds of fighting planes. The Government told me that in doing that I was performing my most useful work in the service of my country."

It is argued that we have passed the stage in the war where national service is necessary. But our soldiers and sailors know that this is not true. We are going forward on a long, rough road — and, in all journeys, the last miles are the hardest. And it is for that final effort — for the total defeat of our enemies — that we must mobilize our total resources. The national war program calls for the employment of more people in 1944 than in 1943.

It is my conviction that the American people will welcome this win-the-war measure which is based on the eternally just principle of "fair for one, fair for all."

It will give our people at home the assurance that they are standing four-square behind our soldiers and sailors. And it will give our enemies demoralizing assurance that we mean business -- that we, 135,000,000 Americans, are on the march to Rome, Berlin and Tokyo.

I hope that the Congress will recognize that, although this is a political year, national service is an issue which transcends politics. Great power must be used for great purposes.

As to the machinery for this measure, the Congress itself should determine its nature — but it should be wholly non-partisan in its make-up.

Our armed forces are valiantly fulfilling their responsibilities to our country and our people. Now the Congress faces the responsibility for taking those measures which are essential to national security in this the most decisive phase of the nation's greatest war.

Several alleged reasons have prevented the enactment of legislation which would preserve for our soldiers and sailors and marines the fundamental prerogative of citizenship — the right to vote. No amount of legalistic argument can becloud this issue in the eyes of these ten million American citizens. Surely the signers of the Constitution did not intend a document which, even in wartime, would be construed to take away the franchise of any of those who are fighting to preserve the Constitution itself.

Our soldiers and sailors and marines know that the overwhelming majority of them will be deprived of the opportunity to vote, if the voting machinery is left exclusively to the States under existing state laws — and that there is no likelihood of these laws being changed in time to enable them to vote at the next election. The Army and Navy have reported that it will be impossible effectively to administer forty-eight different soldier-voting laws. It is the duty of the Congress to remove this unjustifiable discrimination against the men and women in our armed forces — and to do it as quickly as possible.

It is our duty now to begin to lay the plans and determine the strategy for the winning of a lasting peace and the establishment of an American standard of living higher than ever before known. We cannot be content, no matter how high that general standard of living may be, if some fraction of our people — whether it be one-third or one-fifth or one-tenth — is ill-fed, ill clothed, ill housed, and insecure.

This Republic had its beginning, and grew to its present strength, under the protection of certain inalienable political rights — among them the right of free speech, free press, free worship, trial by jury, freedom from unreasonable searches and seizures. They were our rights to life and liberty.

As our nation has grown in size and stature, however — as our industrial economy expanded — these political rights proved inadequate to assure us equality in the pursuit of happiness.

We have come to a clear realization of the fact that true individual freedom cannot exist without economic security and independence. "Necessitous men are not free men." People who are hungry and out of a job are the stuff of which dictatorships are made.

In our day these economic truths have become accepted as self-evident. We have accepted, so to speak, a second Bill of Rights under which a new basis of security and prosperity can be established for all — regardless of station, race or creed.

Among these are:

The right to a useful and remunerative job in the industries, or shops or farms or mines of the nation;

The right to earn enough to provide adequate food and clothing and recreation;

The right of every farmer to raise and sell his products at a return which will give him and his family a decent living;

The right of every business man, large and small, to trade in an atmosphere of freedom from unfair competition and domination by monopolies at home or abroad;

The right of every family to a decent home;

The right to adequate medical care and the opportunity to achieve and enjoy good health;

The right to adequate protection from the economic fears of old age, sickness, accident and unemployment;

The right to a good education.

All of these rights spell security. And after this war is won we must be prepared to move forward, in the implementation of these rights, to new goals of human happiness and well-being.

America's own rightful place in the world depends in large part upon how fully these and similar rights have been carried into practice for our citizens. For unless there is security here at home there cannot be lasting peace in the world.

One of the great American industralists of our day – a man who has rendered yeoman service to his country in this crisis – recently emphasized the grave dangers of "rightist reaction" in this Nation. All clear-thinking business men share his concern. Indeed, if such reaction should develop – if history were to repeat itself and we were to return to the so-called "normalcy" of the 1920's – then it is certain that even though we shall have conquered our enemies on the battlefields abroad, we shall have yielded to the spirit of fascism here at home.

I ask the Congress to explore the means for implementing this economic bill of rights – for it is definitely the responsibility of the Congress so to do. Many of these problems are already before committees of the Congress in the form of proposed legislation. I shall from time to time communicate with the Congress with respect to these and further proposals. In the event that no adequate program of progress is evolved, I am certain that the Nation will be conscious of the fact.

Our fighting men abroad – and their families at home – expect such a program and have the right to insist upon it. It is to their demands that this Government should pay heed rather than to the whining demands of selfish pressure groups who seek to feather their nests while young Americans are dying.

The foreign policy that we have been following – the policy that guided us at Moscow, Cairo and Teheran – is based on the common sense principle which was best expressed by Benjamin Franklin on July 4, 1776: "We must all hang together, or assuredly we shall all hang separately."

I have often said that there are no two fronts for America in this war. There is only one front. There is one line of unity which extends from the hearts of the people at home to the men of our attacking forces in our farthest outposts. When we speak of our total effort, we speak of the factory and the field and the mine as well as of the battleground – we speak of the soldier and the civilian, the citizen and his Government.

Each and every one of us has a solemn obligation under God to serve this Nation in its most critical hour – to keep this Nation great – to make this Nation greater in a better world.

FOURTH INAUGURAL ADDRESS
January 20, 1945

*After shaking hands with Vice President Truman and re-
peating the oath of office after Chief Justice Stone, the
President began his fourth term with a brief speech.*

Mr. Chief Justice, Mr. Vice President, my friends, you will understand and, I believe, agree with my wish that the form of this inauguration be simple and its words brief.

We Americans of today, together with our allies, are passing
through a period of supreme test. It is a test of our courage — of our
resolve — of our wisdom — of essential democracy.

If we meet that test — successfully and honorably — we shall perform a service of historic importance which men and women and
children will honor throughout all time.

As I stand here today, having taken the solemn oath of office in
the presence of my fellow countrymen — in the presence of our God —
I know that it is America's purpose that we shall not fail.

In the days and in the years that are to come we shall work for a
just and honorable peace, a durable peace, as today we work and fight
for total victory in war.

We can and we will achieve such a peace.

We shall strive for perfection. We shall not achieve it immediately —
but we still shall strive. We may make mistakes — but they must never
be mistakes which result from faintness of heart or abandonment of
moral principle.

I remember that my old schoolmaster, Dr. Peabody, said, in days
that seemed to us then to be secure and untroubled: "Things in life
will not always run smoothly. Sometimes we will be rising toward
the heights — then all will seem to reverse itself and start downward.
The great fact to remember is that the trend of civilization itself is
forever upward; that a line drawn through the middle of the peaks and
the valleys of the centuries always has an upward trend."

Our Constitution of 1787 was not a perfect instrument; it is not
perfect yet. But it provided a firm base upon which all manner of men,
of all races and colors and creeds, could build our solid structure of
democracy.

And so today, in this year of war, 1945, we have learned lessons —
at a fearful cost — and we shall profit by them.

We have learned that we cannot live alone, at peace; that our own
well-being is dependent on the well-being of other nations. far way.

We have learned that we must live as men, not as ostriches, nor as dogs in the manger.

We have learned to be citizens of the world, members of the human community.

We have learned the simple truth, as Emerson said, that "The only way to have a friend is to be one."

We can gain no lasting peace if we approach it with suspicion and mistrust or with fear. We can gain it only if we proceed with the understanding, the confidence, and the courage which flow from conviction.

The Almighty God has blessed our land in many ways. He has given our people stout hearts and strong arms with which to strike mighty blows for freedom and truth. He has given to our country a faith which has become the hope of all peoples in an anguished world.

So we pray to Him now for the vision to see our way clearly — to see the way that leads to a better life for ourselves and for all our fellow men — to the achievement of His will, to peace on earth.

UNDELIVERED JEFFERSON DAY ADDRESS
April 13, 1945

While the President was at Warm Springs, he had been working on a speech to be given over the radio to 350 Jefferson Day dinners in various parts of the country. The speech, with the typescript indicating several changes, might have been still further revised had Roosevelt not died on April 12.

Americans are gathered together this evening in communities all over the country to pay tribute to the living memory of Thomas Jefferson — one of the greatest of all democrats; and I want to make it clear that I am spelling that word "democrats" with a small "d."

I wish I had the power, just for this evening, to be present at all of these gatherings.

In this historic year, more than ever before, we do well to consider the character of Thomas Jefferson as an American citizen of the world.

As Minister to France, then as our first Secretary of State and as our third President, Jefferson was instrumental in the establishment of the United States as a vital factor in international affairs.

It was he who first sent our Navy into far distant waters to defend our rights. And the promulgation of the Monroe Doctrine was the logical development of Jefferson's far-seeing foreign policy.

Today, this nation which Jefferson helped so greatly to build, is playing a tremendous part in the battle for the rights of man all over the world.

Today we are part of the vast allied force — a force composed of flesh and blood and steel and spirit — which is today destroying the makers of war, the breeders of hate, in Europe and in Asia.

In Jefferson's time our Navy consisted of only a handful of frigates — but that tiny Navy taught nations across the Atlantic that piracy in the Mediterranean — acts of aggression against peaceful commerce, and the enslavement of their crews, was one of those things which, among neighbors, simply was not done.

Today, we have learned in the agony of war that great power involves great responsibility. Today, we can no more escape the consequences of German and Japanese aggressions than could we avoid the consequences of attacks by the Barbary corsairs a century and a half-before.

We, as Americans, do not choose to deny our responsibility.

Nor do we intend to abandon our determination that, within the lives of our children and our children's children, there will not be a Third World War.

We seek peace — enduring peace. More than an end to war, we want an end to the beginnings of all wars — yes, an end to this brutal, inhuman and thoroughly impractical method of settling the differences between governments.

The once powerful, malignant Nazi state is crumbling, the Japanese war lords are receiving, in their own homeland, the retribution for which they asked when they attacked Pearl Harbor.

But the mere conquest of our enemies is not enough.

We must go on to do all in our power to conquer the doubts and the fears, the ignorance and the greed, which made this horror possible.

Thomas Jefferson, himself a distinguished scientist, once spoke of the "brotherly spirit of science, which unites into one family all its votaries of whatever grade, and however widely dispersed throughout the different quarters of the globe."

Today science has brought all the different quarters of the globe so close together that it is impossible to isolate them one from another.

Today we are faced with the pre-eminent fact that, if civilization is to survive, we must cultivate the science of human relationships — the ability of all peoples, of all kinds, to live together and work together, in the same world, at peace.

Let me assure you that my hand is the steadier for the work that is to be done, that I move more firmly into the task, knowing that you — millions and millions of you — are joined with me in the resolve to make this work endure.

The work, my friends, is peace, more than an end of this war — an end to the beginnings of all wars, yes, an end, forever, to this impractical, unrealistic settlement of the differences between governments by the mass killing of peoples.

Today as we move against the terrible scourge of war — as we go forward toward the greatest contribution that any generation of human beings can make in this world — the contribution of lasting peace, I ask you to keep up your faith. I measure the sound, solid achievement that can be made at this time by the straight-edge of your own confidence and your resolve. And to you, and to all Americans who dedicate themselves with us to the making of an abiding peace, I say:

The only limit to our realization of tomorrow will be our doubts of today. Let us move forward with strong and active faith.

BIBLIOGRAPHICAL AIDS

The emphasis in this critically selected bibliography will be on Franklin D. Roosevelt as president, and of course, on New Deal policies and measures. The vast number of books on World War II have been here limited to those which most closely relate to the President as Commander-in-Chief and as the top foreign policy director.

The books listed are almost entirely in print as of 1970; those few cited without a publisher are currently out of print but are included because of their importance and because most libraries will probably have them.

For additional books see the bibliographies in Burns, Freidel, Leuchtenberg, or Schlesinger.

Asterisks after titles refer to books currently available in paperback.

SOURCE MATERIALS

The majority of documents pertaining to President Roosevelt are housed at the Franklin D. Roosevelt Library at Hyde Park, New York. Opened in 1941, the library has an estimated 20 million documents, with its collection still growing. An addition to the library will be ready in 1971.

A publication, Collections of Manuscripts and Archives in the Franklin D. Roosevelt Library is available. The booklet gives information on the size and availability of the library's 160 collections and can be obtained from Hyde Park.

Increasing interest in various New Deal agencies has caused scholars to consult the holdings of the National Archives. The vast accumulations of documents is slowly being selectively reproduced on microfilm and should be more available to the researcher, especially since the microfilms will be also kept in eleven Federal records centers. A complete list of microfilm is available from the Publications Sales Branch, National Archives Building, General Services Administration, Washington, D.C.

Relatively few of the documents are available in printed form, although, with the publication of the Foreign Affairs series, the number is growing. It would appear that, for the present, the student must depend on the selected documents listed below, or on secondary accounts by scholars who have used the collection at Hyde Park. One important tool, in addition to the official government publications such as Foreign Relations of the United States, would be the New York Times with its invaluable index.

Blum, John Morton. From the Diaries of Henry Morganthau, Jr. 3 vols. Boston: Houghton Mifflin Company, 1959-1967. Also in a revised and condensed one volume edition entitled Roosevelt and Morganthau (1970). Based on the 800 volume set of records kept by the Secretary of the Treasury and close friend of the president, with many revealing quotations and a fine narrative by the author.

Freedman, Max, ed. Roosevelt and Frankfurter: Their Correspondence, 1928-1945. Boston: Atlantic Monthly Press, distributed by Little, Brown & Company, 1967. Justice Frankfurter was one of the President's most valued advisors.

Jacoby, Robert L. Calendar of the Speeches and Other Published Statements of Franklin D. Roosevelt, 1910-1920. Hyde Park: The Franklin D. Roosevelt Library, 1952.

Kilpatrick, Carroll, ed. Roosevelt and Daniels: A Friendship in Politics. Chapel Hill: University of North Carolina Press, 1952. Correspondance between Roosevelt and Secretary of the Navy Josephus Daniels, his chief in the World War I years.

Nixon, Edgar B. ed. Franklin D. Roosevelt and Conservation, 1911-1945. 2 vols. Hyde Park: The Franklin D. Roosevelt Library, 1957. Illuminating on F.D.R.'s continuing interest in conservation.

_____ . Franklin D. Roosevelt and Foreign Affairs. 3 vols. Cambridge: Harvard University Press, 1970. Documents from the Hyde Park collection covering the years 1933 to 1937. The next term is in preparation. Controversy about the documents and their editing and publishing has broken out. Dr. Nixon was on the Hyde Park staff.

Roosevelt, Elliott. F.D.R.: His Personal Letters. 4 vols. New York, 1947-1950. Scheduled for reprint in 1970.

Rosenman, Samuel, ed. The Public Papers and Addresses of Franklin D. Roosevelt. 13 vols. New York, 1938-1950. Reprinted in 1970 by Russell and Russell. The excellent semi-official record by a

longtime associate and close friend. F.D.R., while he lived, took
an active interest in its preparation.

BIOGRAPHICAL TREATMENTS OF ROOSEVELT
AND THE NEW DEAL
The Major Studies

Burns, James MacGregor. Roosevelt: The Lion and the Fox. New York:
Harcourt Brace Jovanovich, Inc., 1956.* Informative but critical
study of Roosevelt in the Thirties.

———— . Roosevelt: The Soldier of Freedom, 1940-1945. New York:
Harcourt Brace Jovanovich, Inc., 1970. The only extensive bio-
graphical account of Roosevelt's foreign policy which has appeared
to date. Excellent scholarship.

Freidel, Frank. Vol. I. Franklin D. Roosevelt: The Apprenticeship.
Boston: Little, Brown and Company, 1952.

———— . Vol. II. Franklin D. Roosevelt: The Ordeal. 1954.

———— . Vol. III. Franklin D. Roosevelt: The Triumph. 1956.

The first three volumes of a projected multi-volume study which,
though, has been moving slowly of late. These take Roosevelt
through 1932, and a fourth volume is reported to cover the single
year 1933 when it appears. Excellent scholarship and interesting
reading.

Schlesinger, Arthur M. The Crisis of the Old Order, 1919-1933.
Boston: Houghton Mifflin Company, 1957.*

———— . The Coming of the New Deal. Boston: Houghton Mifflin
Company, 1959.*

———— . The Politics of Upheavel. Boston: Houghton Mifflin Company, 1960.*

While pro-Roosevelt, Schlesinger's volumes are forcefully expressed and make exciting reading. The completing of the series,
which goes to the election of 1936, has apparently been side-
tracked by the author's more recent interests.

BEST SHORT TREATMENTS

Conkin, Paul K. The New Deal. New York: Thomas Y. Crowell Company, 1967.* A short critique of the New Deal which denies that "pragmatic" correctly describes the Roosevelt philosophy.

Leuchtenburg, William E. Franklin D. Roosevelt and the New Deal. 1932-1940. New York: Harper & Row Publishers, Inc., 1963.* The best short account of the New Deal years.

Moley, Raymond, The First New Deal. New York: Harcourt Brace Jovanovich, 1966. One of the best critical studies by a member of the Brain Trust; also as After Seven Years (1939).

Perkins, Dexter. The New Age of Franklin Roosevelt, 1932-45. Chicago: University of Chicago Press, 1957.* An interesting study by one of the top diplomatic historians of the day.

Tugwell, Rexford. The Democratic Roosevelt. Baltimore: Penguin Books, Inc., 1969.* A 1957 book (with a 1969 preface) by a leading New Dealer. Remarkably objective.

ROOSEVELT IN SPECIAL STUDIES

Of the scores of memoirs by members of his family and other insiders, few are still in print. Included in this list are the two most critical treatments of Roosevelt, by Flynn and Robinson.

Bellush, Bernard. Franklin D. Roosevelt as Governor of New York. New York: AMS Press, Inc., 1955. Shows some of Roosevelt's early social and economic ideas.

Bestor, Arthur, et al. Three Presidents and their Books: The Readings of Jefferson, Lincoln and Franklin D. Roosevelt. Urbana: University of Illinois, 1955.* An insight into the President's mind.

Elletson, D.H. Roosevelt and Wilson. New York: International Publications Service, 1965.

Flynn, John T. The Roosevelt Myth. Old Greenwich, Connecticutt: Devin-Adair Company, Inc., 1948. One of the few available anti-Roosevelt works. Less scholarly than Edgar E. Robinson and should be used with caution.

Freidel, Frank B. F.D.R. and the South. Baton Rouge: Louisiana State University Press, 1965.*

Greer, Thomas. What Roosevelt Thought. East Lansing: Michigan State University Press, 1958.

Gunther, John. Roosevelt in Retrospect. New York: Harper & Row Publishers, Inc., 1950.

Halasz, Nicholas. Roosevelt Through Foreign Eyes. New York: Von Nostrand Reinhold Company, 1961.

Hassett, William. Off the Record with R.D.R., 1942-1945. New Brunswick: Rutgers University Press. Inside story by a White House aide.

Hill, Charles P. Franklin Roosevelt. Fair Saxon, New Jersey: Oxford University Press, 1966.

Lazarsfeld, Paul F., et al. The People's Choice. New York: Columbia University Press, 1944.*

Moscow, Warren. Roosevelt and Willkie. Englewood Cliffs, New Jersey: Prentice-Hall, Inc., 1968.

Nevins, Allan. The Place of Franklin D. Roosevelt in History. New York: Humanities Press, 1965.*

Parmet, H.S. and M.B. Hecht. Never Again: A President Runs for a Third Term. New York: MacMillan Company, 1969.

Perkins, Frances. The Roosevelt I Knew. New York: Harper & Row Publishers, Inc., 1946.* Interesting insights into the Roosevelt character by his Secretary of Labor.

Robinson, Edgar E. The Roosevelt Leadership, 1933-1945. Philadelphia, 1955. The best example of an anti-Roosevelt treatment, marred by some tortured writing and by its one-sided approach. At the moment it seems, not surprisingly, to be out of print.

Rollins, Alfred, Jr. Roosevelt and Howe. New York: Alfred A. Knofp, Inc., 1962.

Roosevelt, Eleanor. This I Remember. New York: Harper & Row Publishers, Inc., 1949.

Sherwood, Robert E. Roosevelt and Hopkins. New York: Harper & Row Publishers, Inc., 1948 (rev. ed.), 1950.

THE NEW DEAL AND NEW DEALERS

This selected list of titles emphasizes books currently in print (1970). although a few classics have been included (no publisher cited). Several new studies are currently in process, especially on the various New Deal agencies.

Albertson, Dean.)Roosevelt's Farmer, Claude R. Wickard in the New Deal. New York: Columbia University Press, 1961. Capable biography of one of the early New Dealers and Henry Wallace's successor as Secretary of Agriculture.

Baker, Leonard. The Duel between F.D.R. and the Supreme Court. New York: Macmillan Company, 1967. Good recent monograph.

Baxter, James P. Scientists Against Time. Cambridge: MIT Press, 1946.* Interesting study of the creation of the Atomic Bomb.

Bernstein, Barton J., ed. Towards a New Past: Dissenting Essays in American History. New York: Random House, 1968.) The essay on the New Deal by Bernstein is a good example of a critique of Roosevelt for his conservatism.

Bernstein, Irving. The New Deal and Collective Bargaining Policy. Berkeley, 1950. Demonstrates Roosevelt's attitude toward labor — sometimes a whole-hearted supporter, at other times not so much.

Brennan, John. Silver and the First New Deal. Reno: University of Nevada Press, 1969.

Brown, Douglas V., et al. The Economics of the Recovery Program. New York: Books for Libraries, Inc., 1968.

Degler, Carl N., ed. The New Deal. Chicago: Quadrangle Books, 1970. A collection of essays printed in the Thirties in the New York Times Magazine, with an introduction by Degler which gives an excellent brief overview of the New Deal.

Eccles, Marriner. Beckoning Frontiers. New York: Alfred A. Knopf, Inc., 1951. A New Dealer's discerning account.

Einaudi, Mario. The Roosevelt Revolution. New York: Harcourt Brace Jovanovich, Inc., 1969.

Ekirch, Arthur. Ideologies and Utopias: The Impact of the New Deal on American Thought. Chicago: Quadrangle Books, 1969.

Fite, Gilbert. George N. Peek and the Fight for Farm Parity. Norman, Oklahoma: University of Oklahoma Press, 1954. One of the best of the studies of a New Deal agency.

Fusfeld, Daniel. The Economic Thought of Franklin D. Roosevelt and the Origins of the New Deal. New York: AMS Press, Inc., 1956.

Goldman, Eric. Rendezvous With Destiny. New York: Alfred A. Knopf, Inc., 1952.*

Hawley, Ellis W. The New Deal and the Problem of Monopoly, 1933-39. Princeton: Princeton University Press, 1965.*

Hofstadter, Richard. The American Political Tradition. New York: Random House, 1948.* The Roosevelt sketch is one of the best.

Hollingsworth, Harold. Essays on the New Deal. Austin: University of Texas Press, 1969.

Humphrey, Hubert. Political Philosophy of the New Deal. Baton Rouge: Louisiana State University, 1970. Mr. Humphrey's masters thesis at Louisiana State.

Ickes, Harold. The Autobiography of a Curmudgeon. New York: Ramdom House Inc., 1948.*

_____ . The Secret Diary of Harold Ickes. 3 vol. New York, 1954.

Jackson, Charles O. Food and Drug Legislation in the New Deal. Princeton: Princeton University Press, 1970.

Jackson, Robert. The Struggle for Judicial Supremacy. New York: Random House Inc., 1941.* Sympathetic account by an insider.

Karl, Barry. Executive Reorganization and Reform in the New Deal. Cambridge: Harvard University Press, 1963.

Lilienthal, David. TVA: Democracy on the March. New York: Harper and Row Publishers, Inc., 1944.*

McFarland, Charles K. Roosevelt, Lewis and the New Deal. Fort Worth: Texas Christian University Press, 1970.*

Martin, Roscoe, ed. TVA: The First Twenty Years. Knoxville: University of Tennessee Press, 1956.

Mitchell, Broadus. Depression Decade, from New Era to New Deal 1929-1941. New York: Holt, Rinehart & Winston, Inc., 1947.* Still one of the best economic studies of the era.

Paris, James Daniel. Monetary Policies of the United States, 1932-1938. New York: AMS Press, Inc., 1938.

Patterson, James T. The New Deal and the States: Federalism in Transition. Princeton: Princeton University Press, 1969. Believes that Federal-State relationships were radically changed by social security and work relief programs.

Phillips, Cabell. From the Crash to the Blitz. New York: MacMillan Company, 1969.

Pritchett, C. Herman. Roosevelt Court: A Study in Judicial Politics and Values, 1937-1947. Chicago: Quadrangle Press, 1969.*

Rauch, Basil. History of the New Deal, 1933-1938. New York: G.P. Putnam's Sons, 1944.*

Rollins, Alfred B., Jr. Franklin D. Roosevelt and the Age of Action. New York: Dell Publishing Company, 1960.*

Rose, Kenneth. The Economics of Recession and Revival. New Haven: Shoe String Press, 1954.

Selznick, Philip. TVA and the Grass Roots. Berkeley, 1953. Now available in a Torch Book (Harper and Row).

Tugwell, Rexford G.   The Brains Trust. New York: Viking Press, Inc., 1968.

———— . F.D.R.: Architect of an Era. New York: MacMillan Company. 1967. Excellent treatments by one of the early new dealers.

Wecter, Dixon. The Age of the Great Depression, 1929-1941. New York: MacMillan Company, 1948.

Wolfskill, George and John A. Hudson. All But the People: Franklin D. Roosevelt and His Critics, 1933-1939. New York: MacMillan Company, 1969.

Wann, .AJ. President as Chief Administrator: A Study of Franklin D. Roosevelt. Washington, D.C.: Public Affairs Press, 1968.

Woods, John A. Roosevelt and Modern America. New York: MacMillan Company, 1959.*

Zinn, Howard, ed. New Deal Thought. Indianapolis: Bobbs-Merrill, 1966.* A volume in the American Heritage Series: an anthology of writings by New Dealers and "social critics" of the period with an introduction by Zinn, a leading attacker of the New Deal for its failure to do enough.

FOREIGN POLICY

The following titles are critically selective, with emphasis on books still in print (1970). The vast amount of writing on the period, especially World War II, including countless memoirs, can be found in such late studies as James McGregor Burns' second volume.

Adler, Selig. The Isolationist Impulse: Its Twentieth Century Reaction. New York: MacMillan Company, 1957.*

_____ . The Uncertain Giant, 1921-1941. New York: MacMillan Company, 1965.* The earlier treatment, while excellent on background is sketchy on the 1930's; the later work remedies this by showing the isolationism of the period.

Baker, Leonard. Roosevelt and Pearl Harbor. New York: MacMillan Company, 1970.

Beard, Charles A. American Foreign Policy in the Making, 1932-1940. New Haven: Shoe String Press, Inc., 1946.

_____ . President Roosevelt and the Coming of the War. New Haven: Shoe String Press, Inc., 1948. Vigorous attacks on Roosevelt's foreign policy which should be balanced by the use of Rauch, Divine, the Langer-Gleason volumes and Burns' newer treatment.

Bishop, Donald G. Roosevelt-Litvinov Agreements: The American View. Syracuse: Syracuse University Press. 1965.

Buchanan, A.R. The United States in World War II. New York: Harper and Row, 1964.* Excellent treatment of the military side of the conflict.

Churchill, Winston S. The Grand Alliance. Boston, 1950.

_____ . Closing the Ring. Boston, 1951.

_____ . The Hinge of Fate. Boston, 1953.

———— . Triumph and Tragedy. Boston, 1953.

Essential for comments on Roosevelt by an admiring ally. The second volume is particularly important on Anglo-American relations.

Dallek, Robert. Roosevelt Diplomacy and World War II. New York: Holt, Rinehart, and Winston, 1970.*

Divine, Robert A. The Illusion of Neutrality. Chicago: University of Chicago Press, 1962.* Good on neutrality legislation.

———— . The Reluctant Belligerent. New York: John Wiley and Sons, Inc., 1965.* A volume of the America in Crisis series which finds American foreign policy sterile and bankrupt in this period, but vacillates between blaming a devious Roosevelt, a cautiously advancing public opinion, and isolationists.

———— . Roosevelt and World War II. Baltimore: Johns Hopkins Press, 1969.* A brief study which critically surveys the President's personal role.

Eisenhower, Dwight D. Crusade in Europe. Garden City: Doubleday & Company, Inc., 1948.*

Feingold, Henry. Politics of Rescue: The Roosevelt Administration and the Holocaust, 1938-1954. Rutgers, 1970. Dismisses efforts to get refugees out of Europe.

Feis, Herbert. The China Tangle: The American Effort in China from Pearl Harbor to the Marshall Mission. Princeton: Princeton University Press, 1953.*

———— . The Road to Pearl Harbor. Princeton: Princeton University Press, 1962.*

The first and third volumes are especially valuable on the Pacific developments; the second a massive study of the interrelationships among the Allied leaders.

Fenno, Richard F., Jr. The Yalta Conference. Indianapolis: D.C. Heath and Company, 1955.*

Ferrell, Robert. American Diplomacy in the Great Depression. New Haven: Shoe String Press, Inc., 1957.* A good overall survey.

Gardner, Lloyd C. Economic Aspects of New Deal Diplomacy. Madison, Wisconsin, 1964. Interesting and challenging view of the diplomacy of the period, though not always convincing.

BIBLIOGRAPHY
215

Guerrant, Edward O. Roosevelt's Good Neighbor Policy. Albuquerque: University of New Mexico Press, 1950.

Heinrichs, Waldo H. American Ambassador: Joseph C. Grew and the Development of the United States Diplomatic Tradition. Boston: Little, Brown & Company, 1966.

Kolko, Gabriel. The Politics of War. New York: Random House, Inc., 1968. Charges that economic interests shaped American foreign policy, especially from 1943-1945.

Langer, William L., and Gleason, S. Everett. The Challenge to Isolation, 1937-1940. New York, 1952.

————. The Undeclared War. New York, 1953.

Surprisingly complete accounts for their date of publication. The authors had access to records not yet opened to most scholars.

Morison, Samuel E. The Two Ocean War. Boston: Little, Brown & Company, 1963. A good condensation of his 14 volume History of the United States Naval Operations in World War II.

Nevins, Allan. The New Deal and World Affairs: 1933-1945. United States Publishers Association, Inc., 1950. A brief volume in the Chronicles of America series.

Pratt, Julius W. Cordell Hull, 1933-1944. 2 vols. New York: Cooper Square Publishers, 1964. Excellent treatment in the American Secretaries of State series.

Range, Willard. Franklin D. Roosevelt's World Order. Athens, Georgia: University of Georgia Press, 1959.

Rauch, Basil. Roosevelt from Munich to Pearl Harbor. New York: Barnes & Noble, Inc, 1950. A short, uncritical study.

Smith, Gaddis. American Diplomacy During the Second World War, 1941-1945. New York: John Wiley & Sons, Inc., 1965.* Brief study in the America in Crisis series.

Snell, John L. Illusion and Necessity: The Diplomacy of Global War, 1939-1945. Boston: Houghton Mifflin Company. A brief account.

Stettinius, Edward R., Jr. Roosevelt and the Russians: The Yalta Conference. Garden City, New York (now Westport, Conn.): Greenwood Publishing Company, 1949. A defense by the Secretary of State at the time.

Tansill, Charles C. Back Door to War. Chicago, 1952. Isolationist treatment, critical of Roosevelt's policies.

Welles, Sumner. The Seven Decisions That Shaped History. New York, 1951.

Wiltz, John E. From Isolation to War: 1931-1941. New York: Thomas Y. Crowell Company, 1968.* Excellent short study.

Wohlstetter, Roberta. Pearl Harbor: Warning and Decision. Stanford: Stanford University Press, 1962.* Relates the failures in our intelligence.

PERIODICALS

The number of articles on Franklin D. Roosevelt is so vast that the use of the usual research tools would take an incalculable amount of time. Fortunately there is a publication which would be of immense help. It is annotated, indexed, and about as complete as humans could ever achieve. The 1967 edition, furthermore, with its 1,339 entries, is presently being updated and is expected to increase the number of entries by some fifty percent.

The Era of Franklin D. Roosevelt, A Selected Bibliography of Periodical and Dissertation Literature, 1945-1966. Compiled and annotated by William J. Stewart. Available from the Franklin D. Roosevelt Library, Hyde Park, New York, 12538.*

NAME INDEX

Acheson, Dean G.,24, 29, 67
Anderson, Marian,55
Arias, Harmodio, 28
Arnold, Henry H., 79
Arnold, Thurman, 52
Avery, Sewell, 94

Bankhead, William B., 51, 65
Barkley, Alben W., 90
Barton, Bruce, 65
Baruch, Bernard,50, 82
Bennett, Hugh H., 39
Berle, Adolph A.,18, 52
Biddle, Francis, 70, 93
Bingham, Robert,23, 51
Black, Eugene R., 37
Black, Hugo L., 49
Blodgett, Eleanor, 1
Bloom, Sol, 96
Boettiger, Anna, 90
    see also Roose-
    velt, Anna
Bok, Edward, 11
Borah, William E.,57
Bowers, Claude G., 23
Bowles, Chester, 88
Brandeis, Louis D., 48
Bricker, John W.,91, 93
Brophy, William A., 95
Browder, Earl, 46, 65, 80
Brown, Prentiss M., 84, 88
Bruenn, Howard G., 90
Bryan, William Jennings 24
Bullitt, William C., 29, 45, 46, 61, 66, 75, 87

Bush, Vannevar, 62
Butler, Pierce, 58, 59
Byrd, Harry F., 92
Byrnes, James F., 70, 82, 83, 85, 98

Camacho, Avila, 85
Cardenas, Lazaro,52
Cardozo,Benjamin,48
Cermak, Anton, 21
Chamberlain, Nevil-
    le, 54, 60
Chiang Kai-shek, 88, 93
Chiang Kai-shek, Madame, 84, 88
Churchill, Winston, 60, 66, 72, 77, 78, 81, 82, 84, 85, 87, 88, 89,92, 93, 95, 97, 98
Clark, Mark W., 89
Cleveland,Grover,32
Cohen, Benjamin V., 34
Collier, John, 24, 95
Conant, James B.,68
Connally, Tom, 96
Coolidge, Calvin, 9
Corcoran, Thomas,34
Coughlin, Charles,37, 38, 45
Couzens, James, 25
Cox,James M., 9,25
Crowley, Leo T., 31, 86, 87
Cummings, Homer S., 21, 55
Cummings, Walter J., 28, 31
Curtis, Charles, 18

Daladier, Edouard, 54
Daniels, Josephus, 6, 7, 8, 23
Darlan, Jean-Fran-
    cois, 83
Darrow, Clarence,32
Davies, Joseph, 46, 55

Davis, Chester C., 84, 86
Davis, Elmer, 81
Davis, John W., 11, 12
Davis, Norman H., 37, 54
Davis, William H., 77, 97
Deane, John R., 93
de Gaulle, Charles, 66, 84, 91, 96
de Kaufmann, Hen-
    rik, 69
Dern, George H., 21, 45
Dewey, Thomas E., 91, 93
Dies, Martin, 52
Dodd, William, 26, 45, 51
Donovan, William J., 71, 81
Doolittle, James H., 80
Douglas, Lewis W., 22, 37
Douglas, William O., 42, 55
Dumper, Arthur, 2

Early, Stephen, 22
Eastman, Joseph, 26
Eaton, Charles A.,96
Eccles, Marriner S., 37
Eden, Anthony, 95
Edison, Charles, 56, 61
Einstein, Albert, 58
Eisenhower, Dwight D., 78, 81, 83, 84 89
Elizabeth, Queen of Great Britain, 53
Emmons, Delos C., 77

Fahey, Charles, 74
Fala (F.D.R.'s dog), 66, 92

217